Future AI Implications for Young Adult Communication

mohd rashid

Abstract

This study explored the potential effects of artificial intelligence (AI) on young adults between the ages of 18 and 25, examining both the positive and negative impact of their use of cutting-edge technologies. The study examined the dynamic interaction between changing technology environments and this demographic's communication patterns, focusing on the urgent need for an updated communication paradigm. The research established the foundation for comprehending and tackling the revolutionary influence of AI on conventional communication frameworks by exploring the historical origins of communication models, namely Berlo's SMCR communication model. The study utilized a qualitative approach that includes research design, population characterization, extensive data gathering, and careful data analysis to support findings. In addition, the research closely examined hypotheses. It placed a high value on reliability, intending to create a solid basis for understanding the complex connections between AI, communication models, and young adults' experiences in both their personal and professional lives. Ultimately, this study aims to contribute to creating efficient communication plans that address the particular requirements and difficulties posed by young adults' adoption of AI technology.

Keywords: challenges, implications, smart devices, artificial intelligence (AI), machine learning (ML), young adults, business communication, decision making, communication model, information technology (IT)

Table of Contents

CHAPTER ONE: INTRODUCTION

Young adults aged 18 to 25 have been raised with direct access to technology in a rapidly expanding digital world (Sher-Censor et al., 2021). Developments in artificial intelligence (AI)-powered technologies have profoundly impacted communication habits among this demographic (Rudko et al., 2021). AI refers to the development of computer systems capable of analyzing data, learning from it, and making predictions or decisions based on that knowledge. Historically, these operations required human intelligence. AI has numerous applications across various sectors and fields.

The pervasive influence of technology impacts almost every aspect of life for young adults. As AI-powered devices continue to proliferate, it is crucial to consider the potential future effects on the behavior of this generation (Rudko et al., 2021). The research proposes a revised communication model based on Berlo's (1960) Source-Message-Channel-Receiver (SMCR) model to address the concerns. The study focused on Torrance, a city in Los Angeles County, California, as the geographical location for sampling and analysis.

As each element consists of five components. While technology may provide many advantages, such as improved connection, informational access, and cutting-edge learning tools, it also poses risks and obstacles (Gözüm & Kandır, 2021). AI-powered devices and usage are essential to comprehending how technology will affect young adults, ages 18 to 25, if society and business managers want to help these young adults develop a positive, balanced connection with technology (Trevisan et al., 2016). The study examined several areas. Identify the areas where technology impacts communication among young adults, such as those who behave at work, outdoors, and home while doing daily chores (Aslan et al., 2022).

While AI-powered technology has its positive outcomes and benefits, the study discussed the negative impacts of AI device usage. The growth of social media platforms, instant messaging, and online gaming has transformed social interaction and communication among young adults (Gözüm & Kandır, 2021). Future social dynamic changes may impact young adult behavior, resulting in greater reliance on virtual connections, potential difficulties in face-to-face communication, and blending of online and offline identities (Aslan et al., 2022).

Therefore, society should recognize the need for a revised communication model to bridge the gap between young adults and their verbal communication patterns (Akyol, 2023). However, balancing technology and other cognitive stimulation is not easy, but it will be necessary. The state of an individual's mind and emotions are included in their mental health (Kasemsap, 2019). It encompasses the capacity to feel, think, and act in a manner that supports a fulfilled life, healthy relationships, and the capacity to overcome obstacles. Emotional wellness is the capacity to identify, comprehend, communicate, and successfully regulate emotions. It entails being aware of one's emotions and having the ability to manage a variety of emotional situations (Kasemsap, 2019).

The continual presence of technology might harm young adults' mental and emotional health. Rising anxiety, sadness, and cyberbullying might be future effects (Papadakis et al., 2022). To minimize any detrimental impacts on mental health, developing digital literacy, teaching young adults about online safety, and promoting appropriate screen-time practices are crucial (Papadakis et al., 2022). Schools and society must consider how young adults' inability to focus, think critically, and participate in deep learning may be impacted by excessive screen usage, passive material consumption, and short attention spans (Akyol, 2023).

Young adults' physical health may suffer in the long run due to increased sedentary behavior from technology use (Akyol, 2023). Future effects might include increased obesity, sleep disorders, and musculoskeletal problems. Addressing these issues will require promoting physical exercise, outdoor play, and adopting good technological habits. As they become increasingly tech-savvy, ensuring young adults understand digital privacy, security, and appropriate online conduct (Papadakis et al., 2022). Considering the above factors, the study aimed to address three key areas to understand the need for a revised communication model.

1. Identify potential obstacles: This part of the study looks for obstacles or problems in the existing communication model that could prevent young adults from communicating effectively directly related to business.
2. Inspire interventions and strategies: This research section concentrates on creating focused treatments and methods to overcome the hurdles identified by introducing a revised communication model to mitigate the consequences to business.
3. Promote well-being and good development: This part of the research highlights the beneficial effects of good communication on the general growth and well-being of the target group, which relatively affects the growth of the business.

After identifying the obstacles, it is essential to investigate the background of these problems, why these challenges occur, and how to mitigate them.

Problem Background

Technology has changed today's younger generation's everyday activities, working or schooling, and social relationships. Understanding the historical background is vital to understanding the difficulties and possible outcomes. There is almost always connectivity and availability of information because of the widespread use of smartphones, tablets, and other digital devices that impact the lives of young adults, the vital point of the study. Young adults growing up in a technologically accessible world have an impact on their behavior, and lack of knowledge can result in inappropriate content exposure, privacy violations, and unethical online activity use (Holland et al., 2021).

Moreover, while still applicable, Berlo's SMCR communication model may face challenges when used with young adults and employees owing to their distinct traits and the quickly changing communication landscape. Young adults may find traditional communication channels less attractive when they cannot assist whenever needed or practical since they increasingly acclimate to digital communication platforms (Darda et al., 2021). The approach may not sufficiently consider how technology is incorporated and the subtleties of digital media communication. Young adults transitioning into the commercial world frequently use large amounts of data from many sources (Loveys et al., 2021).

Furthermore, young adults and professionals are used to using numerous communication channels at once, such as texting, while participating in online meetings (Schonert-Reichl, 2017). Berlo's SMCR Communication Model could miss the intricacy of simultaneous communication across many platforms. Diverse workforces and communication styles result from globalization and the impact of technology (Desai et al., 2022). Discuss how young adults may prefer casual communication approaches in specific work situations, which the standard model fails to address fully (H. Wang et al., 2022). Emojis, instant messaging, and other informal mediums might not easily fit inside the SMCR paradigm.

While acknowledging feedback, the conventional approach may not emphasize the significance of ongoing feedback loops, which are crucial for tailoring messages to these audiences' quickly shifting preferences and requirements (Desai et al., 2022). The SMCR communication model may not consider how various generations understand messages and select communication methods. The model may not adequately emphasize the importance of brainstorming, co-creation, and group decision-making in contemporary communication. Explain how young adults and professionals are comfortable with rapid communication, highlighting that the current model may not adequately address real-time interactions and immediate responses. Both groups value collaboration and interactive communication. A revised version of Berlo's SMCR communication model is required to solve these challenges.

Problem Statement

It is critical to recognize and address any possible difficulties and behavioral effects technology could have on this age level as they develop in an increasingly digital environment (Holland et al., 2021). Technology can create efficient solutions to encourage positive behavioral development and minimize potential adverse effects by recognizing and studying the difficulties of extensive technology use. As a result, the issue statement is to develop strategies promoting healthy and balanced technology use and supporting positive behavioral outcomes. Investigating how technology may affect young adults in the future is necessary (Joshi et al., 2022). The planned investigation includes identifying the challenges and potential consequences in social interaction, cognitive development, emotional well-being, physical health, and digital citizenship. Overall, the study emphasized the necessity of addressing the difficulties or the potential consequences that affect young adults' lives in three significant ways—mental and emotional health, Physical health and lifestyle, and privacy and digital citizenship.

Problem Statement: What are the potential business ramifications of excessive screen time and digital overload of AI-powered devices directly affecting young adults' mental and physical health, cognitive development, and social-emotional learning?

The young adults rely on media for information, guidance, and gratification and how this dependency affects their behavior and decision-making processes. Propose a redesign of Berlo's SMCR communication model to enhance communication efficiency between managers and employees. Berlo's SMCR communication model is a linear communication model that outlines the flow of communication from the sender to the recipient via the message and the selected channel in that order. Although the model's fundamental ideas are still applicable, current workplaces and communication dynamics require specific modifications to increase effectiveness.

The study made Berlo's SMCR communication model more complete and in line with the complexity of contemporary communication by adding a few additional components. The updated model aids companies, business management, managers, and staff to make informed communication choices to foster a more effective and harmonious work environment. As identified, effective communication is a process that involves continuing development and modification.

Purpose of the Study

The study aimed to get a thorough knowledge of technology's potential difficulties, effects, and repercussions on the behavior of young adults aged 18 to 25. The study explored ongoing research to investigate technology's potential impacts on young adults' behavior. The study aimed to understand better several facets of their behavior, such as social engagement, cognitive growth, emotional well-being, physical health, and digital citizenship. Therefore, the research recommended revising Berlo's SMCR communication model to strengthen communications at the business level for future employees aged 18 to 25.

The post-pandemic phenomena have substantially impacted college students' use of AI-powered devices, especially those given by educational institutions (Terziev & Klimuk, 2020). Following the pandemic, there has been a broad acceptance of digital devices and technology, and the face of education has changed. One major factor in this change has been the use of AI-powered devices. It is essential to understand the growing dependence on electronic devices. Transition to remote learning refers to the change in teaching strategies and practices brought about by the COVID-19 pandemic (Taniguchi, 2023).

This phenomenon emerged after the acute pandemic and represented the continued influence and modifications in education—the acceptance and application of online or remote learning techniques as a substitute for conventional classroom instruction (Taniguchi, 2023). During the COVID-19 pandemic, the shift to remote learning became essential to adhere to social distancing protocols and stop the virus from spreading. All levels of education, from primary schools to universities, had to adjust swiftly to the new distance learning formats.

Since the pandemic, there has been a noticeable increase in the usage of AI-powered devices like laptops, tablets, and smart devices that schools give for online learning (Terziev & Klimuk, 2020). Digital classrooms are the second element. Using tools for interactive learning, automated evaluations, and customized educational experiences, educational institutions are progressively incorporating AI-driven technology into virtual classrooms. Governments may administer digital inclusion efforts to furnish persons with devices, internet access, and essential technology resources. The effort may entail direct distribution of devices and internet connectivity, subsidies, or collaborations with commercial groups.

Transition to remote learning under the post-pandemic phenomenon suggests the move to remote learning is a long-term feature of the educational environment rather than a temporary solution (Taniguchi, 2023). Even after the pandemic's severe phase has passed, educational institutions and stakeholders are navigating the opportunities and difficulties presented by remote learning and still view it as a critical component of their overall educational strategy. The utilization of digital materials, online platforms, and blended learning, which blend in-person and remote learning, may all be part of this shift.

In this study, the researcher discussed hybrid learning models, AI-powered messaging apps, analytics for educational insights, the post-pandemic phenomena' drawbacks, gamification, digital literacy, and the need for a communication remodel. Furthermore, to ensure that young adults are ready for the benefits and problems of living in the digital age, it is imperative for studies on this topic to continue and for educational practices to be modified; therefore, explain the necessity to modify Berlo's SMCR communication model.

The Need for a Communication Remodel

The conventional communication model should be updated, and the study reviewed how to do so while considering how AI influences communication habits within this group. The SMCR model developed by Berlo is a well-known paradigm for comprehending communication processes, and its application to the AI-driven communication environment can be insightful (Veczán, 2023). For several reasons, the revised Berlo's SMCR communication model may be crucial to corporate management. The study discussed how clarity and other components can enhance effective communication, understanding, message customization, channel selection, feedback loop, organizational culture, and adaptation to the digital era.

The model urges managers and staff to consider incorporating context, feedback, multimedia, relationships, adaptation, technology, and clarity when communicating effectively. This revised strategy ensures that messages are correctly conveyed, clearly understood, and produce the desired results. Revised Berlo's SMCR communication model can enhance teamwork and collaboration. Building solid teams and promoting cooperation need effective communication (Veczán, 2023). The concept aids managers in developing a more inclusive and cohesive workplace where workers feel appreciated and engaged by emphasizing relationship-building and changing communication techniques. Placing a strong focus on feedback and modification in the model can help to settle disputes. Issues can be dealt with quickly and constructively because of open feedback loops and clear communication routes, which helps keep misunderstandings from getting worse.

Effective communication is essential during organizational transformation (Desai et al., 2022). Because the revised communication model considers context, feedback, and adaptability, managers may advise people about changes in a way that reduces resistance and promotes easy transitions. Business managers may build practical communication skills that energize and excite their employees by comprehending and applying Berlo's SMCR communication model's guiding principles. In turn, this supports successful management and staff advancement. Businesses rely on efficient communication to connect with consumers, comprehend their requirements, and provide superior goods and services (Desai et al., 2022).

A well-used Berlo's SMCR communication model may direct managers to customize their communication methods to various client segments, increasing customer loyalty and satisfaction. Making informed judgments and finding solutions to challenges requires clarity and conciseness in communication (Lutkenhaus et al., 2023). The model's emphasis on concise communication might avoid misconceptions that can result in erroneous decisions. Employee engagement and work satisfaction often rise when employees feel heard, understood, and respected. The model's focus on connections, feedback, and adaptability may help create a productive workplace that promotes employee well-being.

Furthermore, effective communication is essential for handling and directing personnel during crises or emergencies (Lutkenhaus et al., 2023). Context and clarity are two model components that assist in guaranteeing correct and fast communication of vital information. Employees who feel comfortable exchanging ideas and working together on creative initiatives are likelier to do so in a workplace where effective communication is present. The concept encourages the interchange of various ideas and viewpoints by considering multimedia and flexibility.

The researcher examined the study's three key areas.

1. Identify potential obstacles.
2. Inspire interventions and strategies.
3. Promote well-being and good development.

Identify and elaborate on the three critical areas to comprehend the necessity for a revised communication model. The study identified and examined the obstacles brought by the growing influence of technology on young adults. One of the three key areas is understanding the consequences of excessive screen time, social media use, and blending online and offline personas. The research sought to foresee the long-term effects on young adults' behavior by looking at the implications of technology for the future. The study investigated the effect on their social and cognitive skills, as well as their mental and physical health and ethical judgment (Yang & Han, 2020). The study aimed to inspire the creation of interventions, strategies, and educational programs to enhance healthy behavioral outcomes, encouraging young adults' well-being and good behavioral development in the context of technology use, offer advice and ideas to help educators, policymakers, and other stakeholders successfully navigate the digital world and encourage positive technology usage through an effective communication methodology, to understand the possible obstacles and to increase information and to understand about how technology may affect young adult's behavior in the future, with the ultimate goal of promoting positive outcomes by emphasizing the need for a communication model and giving young adults the knowledge and awareness they need to navigate the digital world successfully.

Theoretical and Conceptual Framework

The concept draws on pertinent theories, ideas, and models to direct the research and provide a framework for analyzing the potential behavioral effects of technology on young adults aged 18 to 25.

Social Learning Theory

Albert Bandura created the social learning theory (SLT), a psychological theory that strongly emphasizes how behavior develops through imitation, modeling, and observational learning. By highlighting the significance of cognitive processes, social environment, and other people's influence in influencing an individual's conduct, Bandura's theory goes beyond the confines of classic behaviorist ideas (Bandura, 1971). The idea of SLT, also referred to as modeling or vicarious learning, is at the heart of SLT. The vast majority of individuals aged 18 to 25 pickup knowledge by seeing the actions of others and the results of those actions. These individuals can learn this technique by observing others receive rewards or punishments for their conduct; direct reinforcement is not always necessary.

SLT is frequently called the 'bridge' that unites the cognitive approach with classical learning theory (behaviorism) because it emphasizes the role of mental (cognitive) variables in learning. SLT emphasizes how social factors and observational learning affect behavior (Deaton, 2015). The theory implies that young adults learn through watching and copying others, including technology use (Holland et al., 2021). Additionally, SLT aids in understanding how social influences like peer groups and media role models affect technology usage patterns and behavior. Development psychology can elaborate on the cognitive and psychosocial development phases young adults undergo, as explained by developmental psychology theories (Yang & Han, 2020).

SLT suggests utilizing these concepts to explore the relationship between technology and the developmental challenges and milestones young adults encounter. Overall, SLT suggests the target audience of young adults ages 18 to 25 pickup new skills by watching and copying the actions of others in addition to receiving direct reinforcement. The theory strongly emphasizes the role models play, the significance of cognitive processes, and the interaction between environmental and personal variables in determining behavior.

Media Ecology Theory

Marshall McLuhan's media ecology theory investigates how media and communication technologies affect people's perception, comprehension, and social structure. When McLuhan expressed that the medium is the message, he implied that a medium's qualities (i.e., how information is transmitted) were more important than the material itself (Trevisan et al., 2016). This basic idea states that a communication medium's characteristics and nature significantly impact how people behave and how society functions rather than the particular information it conveys (Islas & Bernal, 2016). Put another way, the medium alters individuals' perceptions of interactions with information. McLuhan projected that electronic media would lead to the creation of a global village.

The global village is defined by the compression of time and distance, enabling immediate communication and connection among people anywhere in the world (Velasquez et al., 2018). This idea foresees the connectivity made possible by contemporary communication technology. According to McLuhan, media influences people's perceptions of and interactions with the outside world by functioning as extensions of human senses. For instance, the phone expands the voice, but the printed word stretches the eye. Researchers are encouraged by media ecology theory to look at the medium itself and its wider cultural and societal ramifications in addition to the content of communication. The theory offers a model for comprehending the dynamic interplay between human experience and media technology, highlighting the revolutionary impact of communication tools on how we live and see the world.

Media ecology theory can examine the dynamic interaction between media and society (Strate, 2002). The theory examines how media and technology influence social relationships, communication, and cultural contexts (Yang & Han, 2020). It aids in comprehending technology's more significant cultural and sociological effects on children's conduct and interactions with their environment. Incorporating concepts from media ecology theory and SLT into corporate operations where young adults are involved can improve communication tactics, organizational culture, and flexibility in response to technological advancements. Organizations that comprehend the social and media dynamics present in their surroundings are more adept at cultivating favorable work environments and navigating the intricacies of the digital terrain.

Research Questions

The study's research questions aimed to learn from young adults about their perceptions, firsthand accounts, and worries surrounding their AI-powered technology usage. When developing tactics to encourage healthy behavioral outcomes in the digital era, these young adults can offer insightful viewpoints that help comprehend the possible ramifications (Yang & Han, 2020). The research questions support the data for the qualitative research. Th format of the research questions are incorporated as follows:

Research Question 1: What are the social-emotional challenges with excessive screen time and digital overload among young adults aged 18 to 25, including the influence on interpersonal relationships, communication skills, empathy, self-awareness, and resilience in the face of digital stressors and distractions?

Research Question 2: What behavioral challenges result from excessive screen time and digital overload among young adults aged 18 to 25, and how do these changes necessitate the existing SMCR communication model?

Research Question 3: What business communication challenges arise from digital distractions and the adverse effects of screen time among young adults aged 18 to 25, and how can businesses adapt the revised SMCR communication model to foster well-being?

Nature of the Study

The nature of the study falls under the descriptive and exploratory study categories. In a descriptive nature, the study aimed to describe and comprehend technology's potential adverse effects, difficulties, and influences on young working people. Descriptive research aims to characterize and exhibit the traits or qualities of a specific occurrence or topic of interest. In this instance, the study focused on comprehending the potential effects of AI-powered technologies on communication among young adults.

A group of young adults would likely gather data to describe the existing communication styles and the degree of AI integration in young adults' lives. They could also look at the various AI technologies and how they affect communication. To create a complete picture of the current situation and potential future effects of technology use among this generation, it tries to gather data and insights from young adults themselves (D. Wang et al., 2021). The study examined several behavioral aspects of young adults, such as social interaction, cognitive growth, emotional well-being, physical health, and digital citizenship.

With an emphasis on foreseeing future effects, it aims to gain new insights and comprehend the intricate interplay between behavior and technology (Terzopoulos & Satratzemi, 2020). Through exploratory research, the study can pinpoint trends, patterns, and potential sources of worry around AI use in young people's communication. Gathering preliminary thoughts and guiding the creation of a redesigned communication model can entail conducting an anonymous questionnaire, holding focus groups with teenagers, and examining recent literature (Tay et al., 2022). The study used a descriptive and exploratory method to produce information and understand how technology and behavior interact, highlighting potential obstacles and windows of opportunity to foster beneficial results.

To address the potential effects of technology on the behavior of young adults, it lays the groundwork for future study and the creation of initiatives, treatments, and legislation (Rice, 2022). Finally, the study can provide a thorough understanding of the present state of AI-powered communication among young adults while examining potential future implications and the requirement for a revised communication model to effectively address these changes by combining descriptive and exploratory approaches (Veczán, 2023).

Research Methods

To comprehensively understand how AI-powered devices influence the behavior of young adults, the research strategy employed two qualitative approaches. The study aimed to explore the impact of excessive smart device usage on the behavior of young adults and gain insights into their personal and professional experiences and perspectives in this context. The plan was to conduct a qualitative research study with a target group of young adults between 18 and 25. The young adult group were contacted through social media platforms such as WhatsApp, Messenger, and Instagram to complete an anonymous questionnaire to help the researcher better understand their experiences and opinions on how smart devices have affected their behavior.

The research occurred in Torrance, California. The objective was to investigate and comprehend the daily use of AI-powered technologies among young adults in the 18 to 25 age range. It is crucial to identify young individuals who frequently engage with AI-powered technologies, such as virtual assistants, recommendation engines, or AI-driven applications (Boerman, 2020). The sample encompassed diverse genders, races, backgrounds, and degrees of familiarity with AI technology. The approach was to conduct online Zoom interviews with the target group, asking eight open-ended questions to gather data.

The eight open-ended interview questionnaires covered three central areas: mental and emotional health, physical health and lifestyle, and privacy and digital citizenship. The questions addressed topics such as time spent using smart devices, personal oversight, experiences, and reported behavioral impacts on young adults. This approach enabled a more nuanced examination of their experiences (Pullen Sansfaçon et al., 2022), helping to understand better the subjective experiences and viewpoints of the target group on the issue.

Torrance in LA County, Southern California was significant as the research location because it highlights its diverse demographic composition and urban character that can provide insights applicable to similar metropolitan settings nationwide. The interview questionnaire can reveal important details about how the participants use and interpret AI-powered technologies. The plan was to collect answers from a representative group of young individuals who often use AI-powered devices, such as virtual assistants, recommendation engines, or AI-driven applications. Below are some essential facts and things to follow about the strategy.

Designing the Interview Questionnaire

The plan used an existing open-source instrument covering AI-powered device usage, young adults, and business implications with five open-ended questions to ask the target audience. It provided a flexible and sufficient time frame for the participants to answer each question so young adults can give accurate, in-depth responses. They shared their own experiences when the interview questionnaire carried open-ended questions that allowed the participants to provide their answers in a lengthy manner without short yes or no answers, which is effective in data analysis (D. Wang et al., 2021).

It may produce high-quality data and cover relevant topics, including questions about technology-related topics, such as social media, online safety, business ramifications, cognitive development, physical health, and emotional well-being. The interview questionnaire asked participants to offer particular examples or stories of their experience at the workplace to support the responses. The interview questionnaire included demographic questions about their socioeconomic status, age, and technical knowledge to further understand the respondents' context.

Participant Selection

Young adults between 18 and 25 are sometimes called 'digital natives' because of their upbringing in a technologically advanced society (Yang & Han, 2020). They are more likely to be accustomed to and at ease with AI-powered devices in their regular routines. This age group is probably primarily comprised of recent graduates who joined a career or students who work while studying. Given the popularity of online and technology-based learning, this group finds it especially relevant to investigate AI-powered technologies in education. The plan is to identify the target audience based on age, career, technological exposure, and other relevant characteristics (e.g., gender, race, and socioeconomic class).

To promote honest replies, young adults can ensure that participation is optional, and that participants' identities and information are kept private. Utilizing a qualitative approach through an online Zoom interview where the young adult groups already exist may gain in-depth insight and narratives, documenting their thoughts and experiences regarding the future consequences of AI-powered technology on young adults' behavior (Yang & Han, 2020). The study also considered contextual factors such as parental guidance and involvement, workplace dynamics and behavior, access to different types of smart devices, educational apps and programs, home environment and rules, and peer, colleague, and sibling influence that may influence how AI-powered smart devices affect young adults' behavior (Chan et al., 2022).

Ethical considerations were a top priority throughout the research project to protect the participants' privacy and well-being. The research methodology was detailed, emphasizing the use of informed consent, confidentiality, anonymity, and online Zoom interviews with an open-ended questionnaire to investigate the impact of AI-powered devices on the behavior of young adults in a qualitative manner. The insight gathered will contribute to the existing body of research on the subject, serving as valuable information for individuals, companies, and their management, professionals, and policymakers.

This knowledge will aid in developing strategies to promote responsible and appropriate smart device usage among young adults (Grabsch et al., 2023). Furthermore, the research outcomes will highlight the necessity for a revised communication model that addresses the challenges and barriers AI-powered technology poses. Instead of adhering to an adaptive communication model, the study introduced the Source-Message-Channel-Receiver (SMCR) model by Berlo. This well-established communication paradigm can be adapted to address the issues posed by AI-powered technology for young adults.

This research can potentially provide young adults with a framework to navigate AI-powered communication effectively. The updated SMCR remodel emphasized ethical content creation, transparency, critical thinking, and feedback integration, ensuring that young adults interact with AI to support their career, well-being, personal development, and ethical principles of personal and professional life where the business will be benefitting at the end of the day.

Data Collection

Using an open-source pre-existing questionnaire as the instrument, the researcher had an audio-only Zoom interview. Communication happened through an email, which sent out the consent and information about the research to make the participant aware of the research and its objective. The researcher can create a concise email introduction by providing instructions on Zoom interviews and requesting the participants to provide their date and time as per their convenience and availability.

Moreover, the researcher should ensure the participants that the platform supports data security and privacy (Rice, 2022). Keeping informed consent clarifies the research's goal, methodology, and potential risks and benefits. Requesting participant permission to attend the online interview is a method of guaranteeing ethical research procedures. The researcher had to decide when to collect feedback but giving participants sufficient time to think and answer the open-ended questions without urgency is better practice. The plan was to send email reminders one day before the online interview. The non-respondents were notified about the interview and send reminders to get feedback on whether they were willing to participate.

The study maintained participant privacy by assuring answers/feedback were kept confidential and anonymized and their personal information was not shared (Rice, 2022). To safeguard data storage and security, the researcher protected the gathered data by maintaining secure storage and abiding by data protection laws. The study ensured that the collected data were stored securely regardless of the data stored method. The plan was to store data in an online database. Then, the researcher implemented suitable safeguards by adding a strong password to prevent unauthorized access or disclosure of participant data.

Data Analysis

To analyze the qualitative research data, the researcher used Python and its libraries to bring out the analysis by using coding, spotted patterns, reoccurring themes, and critical results within the qualitative data. Next was coding, categorizing, and creating a system to classify responses according to the data set's codes, themes, and sub-themes. Categorization aids in systematically organizing and analyzing data (Rice, 2022). Then, the researcher reported the gathered and analyzed results clearly and concisely, supporting the data with participant quotes or examples to enhance credibility via Python visualization tools.

Anticipating Limitations

Anticipated constraints are utilized in qualitative research involving young adults aged 18 to 25, such as subjectivity when recruiting through social media, potential overrepresentation of tech-savvy individuals, and limited generalizability of findings due to geographic and cultural diversity within the sampled population. Honesty and anonymity are other limitations when interviewing young adults (Shirazi, 2023). While fostering more honest replies, anonymity may sometimes cause trust concerns.

Due to worries about the privacy of the young adults' answers, some participants could be unwilling to discuss accurate information, particularly on sensitive subjects. Response bias, too, was a limitation in this research scenario. Young adults with solid beliefs or personal experiences using AI-powered devices may be more likely to answer open-ended questions in an interview. Due to response bias, the sample may be biased toward young adults who hold more extreme beliefs or engage in more extreme actions (E. L. Wong et al., 2022).

The study risked omitting the necessary background to follow up on real-time data without having a way to understand whether the collected data are timely or with past experiences. Another limitation encountered while conducting the research was social desirability bias. Young adults may change their conduct to fit what they believe to be socially desirable or acceptable, mainly while being interviewed (Ratkovic et al., 2022).

Tracking changes in behavior or opinions among young adults can be difficult, especially when utilizing online interviews, according to longitudinal studies (Janvier et al., 2023). To overcome these restrictions, the researcher should carefully consider online interview techniques, maintain transparency regarding the study's goal, and put ethical principles into practice to safeguard the rights and welfare of participants.

Definitions of the Terms

Artificial Intelligence (AI). The replication of human intelligence processes by machines, particularly computer systems, is known as artificial intelligence (AI). These processes include reasoning (using rules to arrive at approximations or firm conclusions), self-correction, and learning (acquiring knowledge and rules for applying it). The vast discipline of AI in computer science aims to build intelligent computers that can carry out activities that generally require human intelligence.

Digital Citizenship. Describes the moral responsibility of using technology and digital resources, including the rights, obligations, and standards of proper conduct in digital settings. To traverse the digital terrain safely, responsibly, and respectfully, people of all ages must practice digital citizenship in today's linked world, where technology plays a crucial part in everyday life.

Digital Literacy. The capacity to use digital platforms and technology to efficiently explore, assess, create, and communicate is known as digital literacy. Being digitally literate is crucial for engaging fully in society, education, and the workforce in today's increasingly digital environment.

Digital Overload. Digital overload, which describes information overload or screen overload, describes the sensation of being inundated with all digital communications, information, and stimuli in day-to-day living. People experience emotions of stress, distraction, and cognitive overload as a result of being inundated with emails, social media alerts, news updates, text messages, and other digital stuff.

Machine Learning. A subset of AI, machine learning (ML), aims to allow computers to learn from data and enhance their performance on specific tasks without explicit programming. ML algorithms employ statistical approaches to identify patterns in incoming data and generate predictions or conclusions rather than depending on explicit instructions.

Media Ecology Theory. Media ecology theory explores the relationships between technology, human culture, and communication medium. It was created by Marshall McLuhan and then refined by Neil Postman and other academics. It sees media as settings that mold and sway people's perceptions, thoughts, and actions. The study of how media technologies impact people, communities, and civilizations across history is known as media ecology.

Social and Emotional Learning (SEL). The term "social and emotional learning" (SEL) describes the process by which people acquire the abilities, dispositions, and knowledge required to recognize and control their emotions, create and meet constructive objectives, feel and act empathetically toward others, build and sustain healthy relationships, and make moral decisions.

Success in SEL is critical for well-being and success in various spheres of life, such as relationships, profession, and education.

Social Learning Theory (SLT). According to psychologist Albert Bandura's social learning theory, people tend to replicate watching, copying, and modeling the actions, attitudes, and feelings of others. Social learning theory emphasizes that cognitive processes like attention, memory, and motivation play a role in learning rather than behaviorism, primarily concerned with external actions and stimuli.

Social Media. Social media includes internet platforms and websites that allow people to produce, share, and communicate ideas, information, and material with other people. On these platforms, users may usually follow and engage with companies, organizations, and public personalities and connect with friends, family, coworkers, and like-minded individuals. Social media now plays a crucial role in modern networking and communication, promoting businesses, fostering social connections, and providing entertainment and news.

Virtual Assistants. Virtual assistants are software-based agents that work for people, usually responding to text input or voice commands. These assistants use natural language processing (NLP) and AI technology to comprehend customer inquiries and offer pertinent actions or replies.

Significance of the Study

The significance of the study on how AI-powered technology will affect young adults' behavior in the future explains several reasons. The study aids in understanding the changing digital environment and its influence on young adults' behavior. The study sheds light on how technology affects a range of facets of young adults' lives, such as the ability to engage socially, grow cognitively, feel emotionally stable, and maintain physical health (Akyol, 2023). The results of the study are to generate policies, rules, and regulations about young adults' technology usage. It can guide companies, businesses, educational institutions, and governments as they develop policies to encourage safe and responsible digital usage (Veczán, 2023).

By highlighting potential obstacles and adverse effects, the study makes creating projects and treatments promoting positive behavioral outcomes easier (Fluck et al., 2020). The study advises creating healthy interactions with technology, supporting digital well-being, and developing responsible digital citizenship, highlighting how the study's findings empower young adults and educators to make informed decisions regarding their use of technology (Brown, 2015). The audience will gain the ability to establish reasonable limits, encourage sensible screen-time practices, and encourage balanced growth in all spheres of life and business (Joshi et al., 2022).

The research recognizes that technology may harm young lives' mental and emotional health, which can eventually bring negative impacts to business, and understanding these consequences makes it possible to create methods to lessen the negative impacts and encourage good mental health outcomes that will support and mitigate business implications (Tay et al., 2022). The study emphasized the significance of critical thinking and digital literacy for navigating the digital environment. It underlines the importance of teaching young adults media literacy, information analysis, and online ethical conduct, which can positively affect business.

By concentrating on the future of business and communication, the research aids society in anticipating and preparing for any problems that could develop as technology develops (Terzopoulos & Satratzemi, 2020). It enables preventive actions to minimize hazards and optimize technology's advantages for young adults' lives at work or in their career. Using the updated SMCR communication remodel, business management techniques can result in more effective operations, staff morale, better customer interactions, and tremendous organizational success. The revised SMCR model offers a thorough framework that handles the complexities of communication in the modern, changing corporate environment, which can directly bring efficiency and effectiveness to businesses.

Overall, the study's relevance rests in its ability to improve knowledge and natural choices and foster favorable outcomes in light of the rapid technology breakthroughs influencing the behavior and growth of young adults by minimizing the effects of mental and emotional health, physical health, and lifestyle, and privacy and digital citizenship on business development. The updated Berlo's SMCR communication remodel offers a thorough framework for examining how young adults' communication is affected by AI-driven technologies to mitigate business ramifications. Understanding the changes in communication dynamics will help stakeholders create strategies using AI's advantages while addressing its drawbacks, ensuring that young adults have a pleasant and empowering experience with digital communication where the entire procedure brings resolution to business growth (Veczán, 2023).

CHAPTER TWO: LITERATURE REVIEW

Young adults face a technological revolution in the quickly changing 21st century, where AI-powered technology is essential to their professional life in their career/workplace. The study explored the complex relationships surrounding young adults and how AI-powered technology impacts the communication cycle, specifying the method or approach used to analyze the data collected in the study of the SMCR communication remodel. Next, it will identify how the change has consequences for the business world. The research examined the complex dynamics of young adults' interactions, communications, and relationship-building in the digital era. Young adults constitute a sizable market population with unique communication preferences, attitudes, and habits. Therefore, this is critical for organizations (Hilty et al., 2023).

Businesses may effectively interact with this population by customizing their marketing tactics, product offers, and customer experiences by understanding these linkages (Koubaa et al., 2023). The emergence of AI-driven technology, such as chatbots, virtual assistants, and customized recommendation systems, has transformed how young adults interact and share information. Businesses use AI extensively to tailor marketing messages, automate consumer interactions, and extract insights from data (Koubaa et al., 2023). The study aimed to determine how AI affects the sender-message-channel-receiver framework by examining the changes using Berlo's SMCR communication remodel to business growth. Businesses must grasp the theory of remodel to properly use AI-powered technologies and enhance young adults' communication strategies for the goodwill of business.

The study aimed to determine how the business community will be affected by the shifts in communication dynamics. Changes in customer behavior, inclinations for specific communication channels, demands for individualized experiences, and the significance of authenticity and trust in brand-consumer interactions are a few examples (Hilty et al., 2023). Businesses must adjust to these developments to be competitive and relevant in the market. Inadequate comprehension and reaction to these ramifications may lead to missed prospects, reduced client contentment, and adverse effects on earnings and profitability (Hilty et al., 2023).

At the same time, the study examined the benefits and drawbacks of the interaction. It clarified the history of Berlo's SMCR communication model and the necessity of modifying it for use in contemporary business and communication. Given the rising prevalence of AI-powered devices, applications, and platforms among young adults, it is critical to comprehend the effects of this all-pervasive technology on their growth and well-being (Baldauf et al., 2021). The literature review examined how AI-powered technology affects young adults positively and negatively to understand complex dynamics. The study provides insightful information for businesses and companies looking to prosper in a world driven increasingly by AI and digital technologies.

Businesses may remain competitive in the ever-evolving market environment by modifying their strategy, improving consumer engagement, and comprehending the intricate connections among young adults and the influence of AI on communication (Hilty et al., 2023). Through a comprehensive analysis of the advantages and disadvantages of AI-driven technology for young adults, the literature review offers a sophisticated comprehension of the intricate dynamics involved. This thorough investigation is crucial for businesses, managers, and administrations and for educating companies, educators, legislators, and tech developers on minimizing any possible risks associated with AI while maximizing its advantages for this population, the young adults.

Navigating Artificial Intelligence for Young Adults' Career Growth

There are some qualities of human intellect that technologies can imitate or replicate. In conventional computing, programs and rules are established and carry out actions. Beyond this, AI-powered technology allows computers to learn from data, see patterns, come to conclusions, and adjust to novel circumstances without explicit programming. Artificial intelligence (AI)-powered technology- performs tasks traditionally but requires human intelligence (Aboueid et al., 2021). AI is the development of computer systems that can analyze data, draw conclusions from it, and forecast or judge anything based on that conclusion.

AI is extensively used across several industries and domains. Young individuals between 18 and 25 increasingly use AI in various contexts (Hilty et al., 2023). AI is powerful because it can process and analyze large volumes of data, identify intricate patterns, and adjust to changing conditions. AI is a rapidly developing field that is changing many facets of business (Ashton et al., 2023). As AI develops, it is critical to consider ethical issues and ensure that young adults develop and use new technologies responsibly for the betterment of business.

AI and its Effects on Young Adults and Business

AI has a wide range of effects on young adults in the business world, impacting their pursuit of education, employment prospects, consumer behavior, communication styles, entrepreneurial activities, and moral concerns. Adopting AI technology and tackling related obstacles can enable youth to prosper in a quickly changing digital environment (Ashton et al., 2023). AI-powered educational platforms and solutions provide personalized learning experiences catered to individual student's requirements and learning preferences. These systems help young adults learn more efficiently by using adaptive algorithms to deliver recommendations, feedback, and information tailored to them. AI-based tutoring programs can also provide in-the-moment help and support, enhancing conventional classroom education where it can finally guide to better business ethics.

AI allows young adults to experiment and develop game-changing solutions across various business sectors. AI technologies lower entry barriers and promote startup growth by enabling the creation of novel goods, services, and business models. Young adults who want to start their businesses or join a career may use AI platforms and technologies to automate tasks, track market trends, and make their businesses successful (C. Y. Chen et al., 2022). In the business environment, AI presents ethical and societal issues that young adults must consider.

A lot of thought and moral judgment must go into issues like algorithmic prejudice, data privacy, job displacement, and the effects of automation on society. The ethical and responsible application of AI technology in the business sector is greatly influenced by young adults (C. Y. Chen et al., 2022). AI is changing the labor market and giving young adults new career options. With the right abilities, plenty of profitable employment opportunities exist in rapidly expanding fields like data science, ML, AI, and robotics. Young adults can obtain well-paying positions in IT businesses, research organizations, and creative startups by developing competence in AI-related fields (Lian et al., 2021). A balanced and inclusive integration of AI in the workplace requires addressing the problems and concerns linked to skill development, job market dynamics, and ethical issues, even as it presents career progression and innovation possibilities.

Young Adults, AI-Powered Devices and Business

Potential problems are associated with the confluence of young adults, their AI-powered device usage, and business. Companies are better positioned to thrive in this changing environment if they comprehend the tastes and habits of young adults, use AI to tailor experiences, handle privacy issues, encourage innovation, and make skill-development investments. Below are the different elements that indirectly influence businesses using AI-powered technologies, as well as both pros and cons. Nevertheless, by implementing a communication remodel, there is a chance that the study will be able to support and mitigate the adverse effects on business through the research results (Haase et al., 2024).

Educational Perspective

With automated grading systems, adaptive tutoring, and individualized learning experiences, AI-powered educational products and platforms benefit young adults. AI-powered chatbots and virtual instructors can help with homework, studying, and test preparation (Ehrlén et al., 2023). AI has changed into intelligent content production tools, language learning applications, and recommendation algorithms for educational materials. By examining their talents, hobbies, and market trends, AI algorithms help young adults plan their careers by suggesting viable job pathways.

Businesses may offer distinctive value propositions and set themselves apart from rivals by integrating AI into their educational platforms and products (Kuang-Tsan & Hong, 2017). Businesses may draw in young adults seeking specialized, effective, and exciting learning solutions by offering automated grading, adaptive tutoring, and customized learning experiences. Companies may provide young adults with professional development and upskilling services by utilizing AI-powered career planning tools and recommendation algorithms (Kuang-Tsan & Hong, 2017). Businesses may assist young adults in finding feasible career trajectories, acquiring appropriate skills, and pursuing career possibilities that align with their interests and objectives by evaluating their abilities, hobbies, and market trends, again benefitting the business.

Marketing Perspective

Companies may benefit from the increasing demand for AI-powered educational platforms and products by creating and promoting creative solutions that meet the learning requirements of young adults. Software developers, online learning platforms, and educational technology firms now have the chance to enter or grow in the education sector. Companies can use subscription-based or licensing models to generate revenue from AI-powered learning platforms and products (Haase et al., 2024). Businesses may create recurring income streams from individual users, educational institutions, or corporate clients by providing access to premium features, content, and services.

AI algorithms collect valuable information on user behavior, learning preferences, and performance metrics and apply it to educational goods and platforms. Companies may use this data to offer individualized insights, actions, and suggestions that will increase the efficacy of their goods and services. Additionally, partnerships, research collaborations, or targeted advertising can generate revenue from aggregated user data. Through partnering with educational institutions, companies may expand their user base, establish a reputation, and encourage the uptake of their platforms and goods (Lian et al., 2021).

Several business opportunities have opened up integrating AI-powered devices into education, including partnerships with educational institutions, data monetization, subscription and licensing models, market opportunities, brand differentiation, competitive advantage, and professional development services. Businesses may promote development, lifelong learning, and good social impact by carefully utilizing AI to fulfill young adults' learning requirements and professional goals (Kuang-Tsan & Hong, 2017).

Job Opportunities

AI-powered search engines connect job openings to young adults according to their tastes and credentials. AI-powered resume screening technologies assist in finding relevant experiences and skills and optimizing resumes for job applications (Nguyen et al., 2022). Companies may benefit from the increasing demand for AI-powered job search engines by creating and promoting cutting-edge products that match young persons (between 18 and 25) with appropriate job vacancies. Recruitment firms, HR technology businesses, and job search portals now have the chance to enter or grow in the employment market.

Companies can use subscription-based or licensing models to generate revenue from AI-powered job search engines. It helps both young adults and businesses. Businesses may create recurring income streams from individual users or corporate customers by providing access to premium features like customized suggestions, enhanced search filters, and career advice services (Haase et al., 2024). The AI algorithms utilized in job search engines gather extensive information on user preferences, skill sets, and job preferences. Companies can use this information to offer individualized career guidance, insights, and job suggestions. Additionally, partnerships, research collaborations, or targeted advertising can generate revenue from aggregated user data.

Employer Partnership

Companies that want to include AI-powered job search engines in their hiring procedures might establish partnerships with employers. Businesses may have targeted young adults access to a broader pool of job prospects, established a reputation, and encouraged young person's looking for work to use their platforms by partnering with firms.

Brand Differentiation and Competitive Advantage: Companies may offer distinctive value propositions and set themselves apart from rivals by integrating AI into their employment search engines. Businesses may draw in young adults looking for practical, individualized, and fast job search experiences by offering features like AI-driven matching algorithms, real-time job notifications, and career development services (Haase et al., 2024).

Professional Development and Upskilling

Companies may provide young adults with professional development and upskilling services by utilizing AI-powered job search engines. Businesses may assist young adults in advancing their careers and realizing their objectives by recommending suitable training programs, certification courses, and networking opportunities based on an analysis of the individual's skills, interests, and professional goals (Haase et al., 2024). Various business relationships, such as market opportunities, subscription and licensing models, data monetization, employer partnerships, brand differentiation, competitive advantage, and professional development services, are presented by integrating AI-powered job search engines into various aspects of job opportunities.

Enterprises may stimulate economic growth, create jobs, and support young adults' professional goals by strategically utilizing AI to meet their job search demands. AI-powered fitness applications may track workouts, create customized training schedules, and suggest foods based on users' unique health objectives. AI-powered mental health applications include mood monitoring, virtual counseling, and tailored coping mechanisms to address anxiety, sadness, and stress (Tai, 2020).

Healthcare and Business

Health monitoring devices with AI capabilities monitor vital signs, sleep habits, and general well-being, enabling young adults to take preventative care (Thai et al., 2023). Companies may benefit from the increasing demand for AI-powered health monitoring devices by creating and promoting cutting-edge products that meet the requirements of young adults (18 to 25) regarding wellness and health. It offers chances for consumer electronics producers, digital health startups, and healthcare technology firms to enter or grow in the healthcare industry (Hekkala & Hekkala, 2021).

Businesses may create recurrent income streams by providing healthcare providers or individual consumers access to premium features like tailored suggestions, enhanced analytics, and telehealth services. Companies can use this data to offer suggestions, treatments, and insights into individualized health. Additionally, partnerships, research collaborations, or targeted advertising can generate revenue from aggregated user data (Hekkala & Hekkala, 2021).

Partnerships with Healthcare Providers

Companies may collaborate with healthcare providers to create partnerships that will allow them to include health monitoring devices with AI capabilities into their workflows for patient care and administration. Businesses may reach a broader patient base, establish a reputation, and encourage young adults looking for preventative healthcare solutions to embrace their devices by working with hospitals, clinics, and healthcare systems. By integrating AI into health monitoring products, companies may set themselves apart from rivals and provide distinctive value propositions (Thai et al., 2023).

Businesses may draw in young adults looking for proactive, data-driven, and comprehensive approaches to healthcare management by offering features like AI-driven health insights, tailored wellness programs, and predictive analytics. Companies may provide healthcare professionals and caregivers with professional development and training using AI-powered health monitoring equipment (Hekkala & Hekkala, 2021). Businesses may enable healthcare practitioners to successfully deploy and integrate AI-powered devices into their patient care procedures by offering education and training on AI technology, data interpretation, and remote monitoring methods.

Integrating AI-powered devices with a remodeled communication system into various healthcare domains presents business opportunities. These include partnerships with healthcare providers, subscription and licensing models, data monetization, market opportunities, brand differentiation, competitive advantage, and professional development services (Tai, 2020). Companies that use AI strategically to meet the requirements of young adults in terms of wellness and health may increase sales, enhance patient outcomes, and support population health management initiatives.

Recommendation Systems and Business

Recommendation systems powered by AI algorithms are present on social media sites, offering young adults recommendations for relevant material, relationships, and ads (Liang et al., 2024). With the help of AI-powered recommendation algorithms, social media networks may profit from targeted advertising. These systems can deliver targeted adverts to young adults between 18 and 25 by evaluating user behavior, interests, and demographics. It increases the possibility of engagement and conversion for advertisers. For social media companies, this generates a profitable ad revenue business model.

Recommendation systems employ AI algorithms to collect valuable user preferences, activities, and interaction data. Social media companies may profit from this data by giving marketers, advertisers, and third parties access to insights, analytics, market research, trend analysis, and audience, and by examining how segmentation utilizing aggregated user data can offer social media companies fresh revenue streams (Liang et al., 2024). Social media companies may use recommendation algorithms driven by AI to provide premium or subscription-based services. For instance, premium users could access more sophisticated recommendation systems, exclusive material, or improved personalization choices. Social media firms may earn recurring money from young adults who desire a more customized and individualized social media experience by offering value-added services (Liang et al., 2024).

Social Media Platforms and Business

Social media platforms may establish collaborations and partnerships with influencers, companies, and content providers to use AI-powered recommendation systems (Hekkala & Hekkala, 2021). Social media firms may generate money by partnering with relevant stakeholders and monetizing user interaction through sponsored content, collaborations, and affiliate marketing initiatives.

Enhanced User Engagement and Retention: By offering relevant and customized suggestions for young adults between 18 and 25, AI-powered recommendation systems improve user engagement and retention on social media platforms.

These systems boost user happiness, time spent on the platform, and overall engagement metrics by exposing relationships, content, and adverts that match user interests and preferences. It eventually leads to long-term user retention and loyalty. Social media platforms may draw in companies and marketers looking to target young adults between 18 and 25. Social media firms may monetize user engagement and foster brand relationships by providing advertising options, sponsored content placements, and influencer collaborations (Hekkala & Hekkala, 2021). These agreements can result in reciprocal benefits such as increased income and brand visibility.

Incorporating AI-powered recommendation systems into social media platforms offers a range of business opportunities, such as increased user engagement and retention, data monetization, subscription and premium features, partnerships and collaborations, advertising revenue, and brand partnerships and advertising opportunities (Hekkala & Hekkala, 2021). Companies may increase income, boost user engagement, and improve the general user experience for young adults (18–25) on social media platforms by carefully utilizing AI-driven recommendation systems.

Conversational AI-Powered Devices and Business

Among young individuals between 18 and 25, conversational AI-powered devices like virtual assistants and smart speakers are becoming increasingly common. Businesses that cater to young adults between the ages of 18 and 25 have a lot of potential thanks to conversational AI-powered products. By utilizing marketing, e-commerce, customer service, and data analytics platforms, companies may interact with their target audience in novel and creative ways, stimulating expansion and improving buyers' satisfaction (Thai et al., 2023). However, firms must put privacy and trust first to maintain good ties with young customers.

Chatbots and Virtual Assistants

Chatbots and AI-powered virtual assistants improve user experiences on messaging apps by offering entertainment, customer service, and tailored suggestions. AI-generated content gives young adults artistic and creative ways to interact with digital media and express themselves through music, art, and films. AI-powered chatbots and virtual assistants enhance messaging app user experiences by offering young adults between 18 and 25 personalized recommendations and immediate customer support (Thai et al., 2023). Companies may interact with consumers in real-time, respond to questions, fix problems, and make tailored suggestions using these AI-powered solutions. It will increase customer happiness and loyalty and eventually lead to growth in the business.

Impacts on the Communication Process

Artificial intelligence (AI)-driven chatbots and virtual assistants lower the need for human participation in customer support operations, which helps organizations save money and operate more efficiently. Businesses may enhance profitability and scalability by streamlining processes, reducing personnel needs, and allocating resources more wisely by automating routine queries and support duties (Tai, 2020). Artificial intelligence-powered chatbots and virtual assistants collect helpful information about user interactions, preferences, and habits. Companies may utilize this data to learn about user preferences, wants, and trends, which will help them with product development, marketing plans, and customer engagement programs. Additionally, companies may provide additional revenue streams by monetizing aggregated user data through partnerships, targeted advertising, or research collaborations (Thai et al., 2023).

AI-generated content gives young adults between 18 and 25 imaginative and artistic methods to engage with digital media and express themselves via movies, music, and art. AI algorithms can provide individualized playlists, personalized content recommendations, and customized creative experiences that speak to each person's unique interests and preferences by examining their preferences and behavior. It improves user happiness, retention, and engagement on messaging applications, eventually boosting sales and fostering brand loyalty for companies and the entire business (Ghoreishi, 2023).

Companies may set themselves apart from rivals and provide distinctive value propositions by including chatbots, virtual assistants, and AI-generated content in their messaging applications. Businesses may attract young adults (18 to 25) who value ease, fun, and creativity in their digital interactions by offering creative and customized user experiences. By doing this, companies establish themselves as industry leaders in messaging apps and boost user engagement and brand loyalty.

Chatbots, virtual assistants, and AI-generated content can be integrated into messaging apps to offer a range of business benefits, such as improved customer engagement, cost and efficiency savings, data collection and insights, personalized content and recommendations, and competitive advantage and brand differentiation (Ghoreishi, 2023). Businesses may boost revenue growth, build brand loyalty, and keep a competitive advantage in the digital marketplace by carefully utilizing AI-powered tools and content to improve user experiences for young adults aged 18 to 25.

Budgeting Applications and Business

AI-powered budgeting applications examine spending patterns, spot chances for savings, and offer tailored financial guidance to assist young adults in managing their money wisely. AI-powered investment systems provide automated risk assessment, portfolio management, and trading techniques catering to each user's risk tolerance and financial objectives (Batool & Yosuf, 2023). The financial assets of young adults are protected by AI-based fraud detection systems, which also improve security measures for digital payments, online banking, and transactions. Budgeting apps with AI capabilities examine users' spending trends and money management practices to offer recommendations and insights that are specific to them.

These apps can provide young adults between 18 and 25 with personalized financial advice based on their unique interests and behaviors, enabling them to reach their financial objectives and manage their money more skillfully. By examining spending habits and identifying areas where users may reduce expenses or make more economical selections, AI algorithms used in budgeting software can find potential for savings. Through the visualization of possible savings, these apps enable young adults to make well-informed decisions and make the most of their financial resources (Ghoreishi, 2023). AI-powered investment systems provide automated risk assessment, portfolio management, and trading strategies customized to each user's financial goals and risk tolerance, which supports business in the long term.

These systems use ML algorithms to evaluate investment risks and market trends and optimize portfolio allocations to minimize risks and maximize returns for young adults between 18 and 25. Financial management solutions enabled by AI help young adults make data-based, more effective financial decisions. Through real-time insights, predictive analytics, and practical advice, these technologies assist users in navigating intricate financial environments and taking advantage of growth and wealth accumulation possibilities for business goodwill.

AI algorithms are employed in investing systems and budgeting apps to continually learn from and adjust to customers' shifting financial demands and preferences (Chu et al., 2023). These systems can improve over time by including feedback loops and iterative procedures, giving young adults more precise and pertinent advice as they navigate the financial world. AI-powered technologies enable young adults to take charge of their financial destiny and develop financial literacy by providing individualized financial counsel and insights (Chu et al., 2023). By being thoroughly aware of their spending patterns, investment possibilities, and long-term goals, young adults may make well-informed financial decisions consistent with their beliefs and aspirations, which is the end goal of the study by implementing a communication remodel to mitigate the communication barriers for the betterment of business.

For young adults between 18 and 25, integrating AI-powered budgeting apps and investing systems into financial management offers tailored financial assistance, optimum savings possibilities, effective decision-making, ongoing learning, and empowerment. In a financial environment that is becoming more complicated and dynamic, these technologies enable consumers to manage their money sensibly, accumulate wealth, and attain financial stability. AI significantly impacts young adults' lives to maintain workplace and business ethics by providing tailored experiences, boosting productivity, and making decision-making easier in various contexts (Chu et al., 2023).

To guarantee AI is used responsibly and moderately among young adults, it is crucial to identify the communication gaps and bring up a communication remodel to bridge the gap, which is the main objective of the study. Develop the existing business world with all positivity by using Berolo's SMCR communication model where the target audience will be beneficial through the usage of AI-powered devices without a digital overload instead with an understanding of AI-powered device usage in an effective communication remodel for their well-being at the same time, to the business (Chu et al., 2023).

Components of Artificial Intelligence and Business

Several components of AI may significantly impact business communication. By integrating the AI components listed below into corporate communication strategies, young adults and firms may improve productivity, efficiency, and effectiveness while cultivating improved connections, engagement, and cooperation with internal and external stakeholders. It is imperative to consider ethical and privacy issues to guarantee transparency, accountability, and the appropriate application of AI technology in communication practices.

Machine Learning

ML techniques, a subset of AI, are used by many AI-powered technologies to allow systems to learn from data without the need for explicit programming. As a result, they can gradually raise their level of performance (Islam et al., 2024). Young adults will benefit from ML in catering to the business. In other words, there are positive outcomes for ML in business. Young adults may concentrate on more strategic and creative areas of their employment by using ML algorithms to automate monotonous activities (Sitaula et al., 2023). Businesses might make more accurate and well-informed judgments using ML to enable data analysis instead of intuition when making decisions.

ML algorithms may lower operating expenses, increase efficiency, and optimize processes—all advantageous for young adults launching or managing businesses (Hultgren et al., 2022). Young adults can get a competitive edge in the market by using ML technologies early on, particularly in fields where innovation is essential. Young adults might be empowered to predict future demands and modify their tactics accordingly by using ML to forecast trends, client behavior, and market shifts.

Components and Application

Technical knowhow is needed to implement ML solutions, which might be difficult for young adults without a data science or programming background. It can be costly to develop and operate ML systems, including the expenditures of infrastructure, data collecting, and recruiting qualified personnel (Boustani et al., 2022). Because ML depends heavily on massive datasets, it raises worries regarding data privacy and security breaches. It may be especially troublesome for young adults who handle sensitive data. Biases in the training data are maintained by ML algorithms, which might result in discrimination, unjust outcomes, and moral conundrums.

Because ML models are only as good as the data on which they are trained, ML predictions may not be as accurate or reliable when the data are low quality. Young adults must traverse complicated regulatory frameworks that often differ between businesses and locations and control data usage and ML applications (Zhang et al., 2023). Overall, ML has much to offer young adults in the corporate world, but it also comes with many obstacles to realizing its full potential.

Impacts on the Communication Process

In the corporate world, young people between 18 and 25 are impacted by ML, which presents both possibilities and difficulties impacting enterprises. First, young adults may interact with coworkers, clients, and stakeholders more skillfully thanks to ML algorithms, which enable individualized communication methods catered to individual tastes and habits. By using ML algorithms to analyze large datasets and find patterns and trends, young adults may create personalized messages that appeal to specific groups (Bae et al., 2023). It improves communication effectiveness and builds better connections. Furthermore, chatbots and virtual assistants driven by ML simplify communication processes, allowing young adults to effectively handle questions, plan meetings, and obtain pertinent information instantly.

These automated solutions eventually improve corporate effectiveness and efficiency by increasing productivity and allowing young adults to concentrate on high-value work (Bae et al., 2023). It is important to highlight the potential risks of ML that need to be effectively managed, notwithstanding its numerous advantages. As massive volumes of personal data are collected and analyzed by ML systems to customize communication methods, privacy problems surface. To avoid legal repercussions and harm to a company's reputation, young adults must carefully balance using data-driven insights and upholding individuals' right to privacy. It includes adhering to regulatory frameworks like the General Data Protection Regulation (GDPR).

Furthermore, if ML algorithms are not correctly calibrated and controlled, their complexity may result in bias and false information. To reduce the possibility of spreading false or biased information, young adults must critically assess the output of ML-powered systems (Bae et al., 2023). It will protect the integrity of communication channels and preserve stakeholder confidence. ML presents a unique opportunity for young adults in the corporate world to improve communication processes and drive business outcomes.

However, proper assessment and management of the related challenges are necessary to realize this potential fully. Young adults can confidently traverse the changing communication environment by properly and ethically utilizing the power of ML. It will eventually help organizations succeed and remain viable if AI-powered device usage issues are mitigated.

Natural Language Processing

NLP makes it possible for apps to communicate with users in a style that is more like that of a person, which makes tasks like sentiment analysis, language translation, and speech recognition easier (Bou-Matar et al., 2023). From a business standpoint, NLP presents young adults with several benefits and drawbacks. With NLP, young adults can swiftly evaluate and comprehend enormous amounts of text data, which helps them communicate effectively with consumers, clients, and coworkers in a business environment (Chowdhary, 2020).

Business Decisions of Natural Language Processing

By analyzing social media, reviews, and customer feedback, young adults can make wise business decisions using NLP algorithms to assess sentiment toward goods, services, and brands.

Using NLP algorithms to analyze social media postings, online reviews, and customer feedback, young adults may determine public opinion about products, services, and brands. Recognizing strengths and weaknesses in customer sentiment enables focused enhancements or modifications to customer service procedures, product offers, and marketing tactics (Chowdhary, 2020).

Young adults may use NLP algorithms to glean insightful information on the features, usability, and general satisfaction of products from client comments and explain how information derived from sentiment analysis and engagement levels, facilitated by NLP algorithms, can guide product development processes, aid in decision-making regarding new product launches or improvements aligned with consumer preferences, and assess the effectiveness of marketing strategies among young adults, thereby enhancing campaign performance and ROI through message refinement, precise targeting, and channel selection.

Young adults may actively manage and protect their brand's reputation by employing NLP algorithms to track social media discussions and online reviews. Real-time detection and handling of negative sentiment or possible crises enables prompt responses and damage control strategies, maintaining the credibility and confidence of the brand (Fanni et al., 2023). Companies may modify their approaches and products appropriately through constant awareness of evolving customer inclinations and market conditions, guaranteeing their pertinence and competitiveness in the industry (Fanni et al., 2023).

Effective business decisions enabled by NLP algorithms essentially utilize sentiment analysis insights to improve client experiences, stimulate creativity, maximize marketing expenditures, and preserve a favorable brand reputation. By utilizing NLP technology to make data-driven choices, young adults may position their enterprises for success in an increasingly competitive and dynamic economy (Fanni et al., 2023).

Effects of Natural Language Processing

Real-time language translation made possible by NLP helps young adults interact more successfully with partners, clients, and customers worldwide (Weeks et al., 2023). Young adults performing research or reviewing reports might save time and effort using NLP algorithms to summarize long texts, extract meaningful information, and create insights. NLP models help young adults with content production activities and uphold a consistent brand voice by producing content like product descriptions, articles, and marketing materials.

Based on the training data, NLP algorithms may display biases that provide unfair results or discriminating words, which can harm young adults' reputations and brand image (Braddock et al., 2023). Putting NLP solutions into practice might be difficult for young adults without prior experience in ML, linguistics, or programming. NLP models may be unable to keep up with growing demand or amounts of data, which might cause processing delays or performance problems, particularly for young adults in charge of large-scale operations.

The credibility of young adults may be weakened by NLP systems' inability to handle ambiguity, slang, or context comprehension, which can result in errors or misinterpretations in analysis or communication. Developing and maintaining NLP systems may be expensive for young adults in business, involving infrastructure costs, data labeling, model training, and continuous improvement. Despite these obstacles, NLP has many options for young business adults to improve communication, automate processes, and extract insights from textual data (He et al., 2022). Young adults may use NLP to effectively drive innovation and growth in their enterprises by addressing the related risks and investing in the appropriate resources and skills.

Computer Vision

AI-driven devices with computer vision functionalities can evaluate and decipher visual data from the outside environment. It covers a variety of applications, including object and face identification and picture recognition. From a commercial standpoint, AI-driven devices with computer vision have several benefits and drawbacks for young adults (Fein et al., 2007). Young adults may focus on more strategic parts of their profession by using AI-driven devices with computer vision to automate repetitive chores like data input, inventory management, and document processing. High-precision visual data analysis is possible using computer vision algorithms, which lowers mistakes and boosts accuracy on tasks like object identification, picture categorization, and quality control.

With the help of AI-powered devices, young adults can swiftly evaluate vast amounts of visual data and derive essential trends, insights, and patterns from photos or videos to aid in corporate decision-making. By studying facial expressions, gestures, and behavior, computer vision technology may personalize consumer encounters and help young adults customize products, services, and marketing campaigns to their preferences (Hilty et al., 2023). AI-driven computer vision surveillance systems can improve workplace safety by recognizing real-time security risks, tracking adherence to safety procedures, and detecting dangers. With computer vision, young adults may create cutting-edge goods and services that drive corporate development and distinction. Examples include virtual try-on experiences, augmented reality (AR) apps, and interactive marketing campaigns.

Concerns of Computer Vision

AI-driven computer vision equipment raises concerns about surveillance, face recognition, and data collecting, potentially undermining shareholder, employee, and consumer confidence. Based on the training data, computer vision algorithms may display biases that result in unjust outcomes or discriminatory behaviors, especially regarding recruiting, promotion, and consumer profiling (Hultgren et al., 2022). Implementing AI-driven devices with computer vision requires technical competence in ML, computer vision, and software development for young adults without specialized training or resources. Young adults in business may be unable to afford the high development and deployment costs associated with AI-driven computer vision devices, including hardware, software, training data, and continuing maintenance.

To ensure compliance and reduce legal risks, young adults must traverse regulatory frameworks such as data protection laws, privacy rules, and industry standards that regulate the usage of AI-driven devices with computer vision. Since computer vision models may only be as effective as the data they are trained on, biased or low-quality training datasets can compromise the accuracy and dependability of AI-driven systems, which can harm the performance and reputation of businesses (Imtiaz et al., 2021). Overall, even though young adults in business may profit significantly from AI-driven devices with computer vision, it is critical to address the dangers and obstacles that come with their use to ensure their responsible and ethical deployment and protect both corporate interests and social well-being.

Speech Recognition

Spoken language is translated into written form using AI-powered speech recognition technology. Voice-activated programs, transcription services, and virtual assistants all use this. From a commercial standpoint, AI-powered voice recognition technology has several benefits and drawbacks for young adults (Straand et al., 2024). Thanks to AI-powered speech recognition technology, young adults can now dictate text instead of typing it, which saves time and boosts productivity—especially for jobs like taking notes, writing emails, and generating documents.

Young adults with disabilities or mobility limitations can connect with digital devices and apps more efficiently in the workplace thanks to speech recognition technology, which enhances accessibility.

Impacts of AI-Powered Speech Recognition

Speech recognition technology allows young adults to interact with technology hands-free, allowing them to walk about, multitask, or engage in other activities (A. Kang et al., 2023). AI-driven voice recognition technology lowers learning curves and boosts young adult user satisfaction by offering a more intuitive and natural method to engage with devices and applications. Multilingualism and accent detection are supported by speech recognition technology, which makes it easier for young adults from different linguistic backgrounds to collaborate and communicate in international business settings.

Regardless of their location or availability of conventional input devices, young adults may engage more productively in virtual meetings, conferences, and cooperative work sessions thanks to speech recognition technology (T. L. Lee et al., 2023). For young adults with accents or those with speech difficulties, AI voice recognition equipment may not be able to effectively record speech, particularly in loud surroundings, which might result in inaccurate transcriptions. Speech recognition technology in commercial contexts raises privacy issues over gathering and storing audio data and possibly misusing or accessing sensitive information without authorization.

To uphold ethical standards and trust in business practices, young adults must consider the ethical implications of speech recognition technology, including ensuring transparency, consent, and fairness in its deployment, especially in contexts involving sensitive or confidential information (Matić et al., 2022). Young adults in business may profit significantly from AI-powered voice recognition technology, but to fully realize its potential and guarantee its ethical and responsible usage in work environments, it is imperative to tackle the dangers and obstacles that come with it.

Voice Spoofing

Voice spoofing, in which hackers impersonate authorized users to obtain unauthorized access to systems or sensitive data, is one security concern associated with AI-powered speech recognition technology that might endanger young adults and their companies. To ensure smooth adoption and integration, young adults may need to invest time and money in customization, integration, and training (Cox, 2021). Technical obstacles may arise when integrating voice recognition technology into corporate systems and workflows. Due to its reliance on cloud-based services and internet access for processing and analysis, speech recognition technology is vulnerable to service outages and network interruptions, which may limit the technology's usefulness for young adults.

Autonomous Systems

AI is essential to developing autonomous systems, including robots, drones, and self-driving automobiles. Without human assistance, these systems move, sense their surroundings, and make judgments using AI algorithms. Robotics, drones, and self-driving cars are examples of autonomous systems for which AI is essential. From a commercial standpoint, this development has benefits and drawbacks for young adults (P. Lee et al., 2022). AI-powered autonomous systems can do jobs more quickly than young adults, increasing productivity and lowering company operating costs. AI-driven autonomous systems can reduce workplace accidents, minimize human error, and reduce hazards related to hazardous operations, improving safety across various sectors.

A considerable workforce is no longer needed because autonomous technologies can replace or complement human labor in various functions. It may result in significant savings on pay, benefits, training, and other related personnel expenses. Autonomous systems can maximize resource allocation and use through data analysis and real-time monitoring. Autonomous robots, for instance, can reduce material waste in manufacturing by carefully regulating production procedures. Autonomous cars can optimize logistics routes, minimizing fuel consumption and transit time. Businesses can save money over the long run using autonomous systems since they can minimize personnel expenses and maximize resource utilization while improving asset management (Boustani et al., 2022).

Autonomous Systems for Business Savings

The adoption of self-driving technology signals a paradigm shift in several industries with several advantages (U. Lee et al., 2014). Labor costs decrease as intelligent robots take over jobs that were previously completed only by humans, maximizing operating costs. At the same time, energy efficiency is increased by installing self-sufficient systems, which reduces utility costs. Additionally, as autonomous systems simplify inventory control and lessen the financial strain associated with surplus stock, goods management experiences a revolution. Safety and risk reduction are significantly increased, especially in dangerous situations when accidents are reduced by using autonomous systems (U. Lee et al., 2014).

In addition to generating financial benefits, this comprehensive integration pushes enterprises toward increased sustainability and productivity. AI allows autonomous systems to scale their operations quickly, which helps companies grow their capabilities and respond to shifting needs without significantly investing in new human resources. Creating autonomous systems promotes creativity and propels technical progress, allowing young adults to create novel goods, services, and economic strategies (Nguyen et al., 2022).

Early Adoption of AI-Driven Autonomous Systems

Early adoption of AI-driven autonomous systems gives businesses a competitive edge in the market and helps them draw in top talent, investors, and consumers by providing innovative solutions and increased efficiency (Nguyen et al., 2022). It may be financially difficult for young adults and startups to make the significant upfront investments in infrastructure, training, research, and development needed to design and implement AI-driven autonomous systems. Because autonomous systems must adhere to intricate regulatory frameworks covering safety, responsibility, privacy, and ethical problems, organizations must skillfully manage legal obligations and compliance difficulties.

Ethical Implications

Because AI is being used in autonomous systems, corporations must appropriately address the ethical implications of this technology. These concerns include accountability, transparency, prejudice, and job displacement (Sikström et al., 2023). Technical complexity, such as algorithm development, sensor integration, software testing, and cybersecurity, are involved in designing and sustaining AI-driven autonomous systems, and they may call for specific knowledge and resources. Even with safety advancements, AI-driven autonomous systems still carry some risk of failure, mistakes, or unforeseen repercussions. These might result in mishaps, injuries, or property damage, affecting a company's liabilities and reputation.

Businesses must address the ethical implications of AI in autonomous systems, particularly concerning young adults (18 to 25 years old), who are critical users of AI-driven goods and will play a significant role in establishing social norms and values as future leaders.

First and foremost, businesses should prioritize accountability and openness in the development and application of AI. Young adults are better equipped to judge how to use AI-driven technologies when they are given explicit explanations of how these algorithms work and any potential biases or restrictions (U. Lee et al., 2014). It also helps to build trust in these technologies.

Second, companies should actively involve young adults in moral conversations about AI, asking them for their opinions and views on how these technologies affect human rights, privacy, and society. By integrating multiple ideas and opinions, corporations may guarantee that their AI activities align with ethical principles and social values (Sitaula et al., 2023). This approach can help mitigate possible risks and promote responsible usage of AI.

Additionally, businesses must fund AI literacy and education initiatives aimed at young adults, giving them the information and analytical abilities to negotiate AI technology's ethical challenges successfully. Corporations can foster a generation of responsible AI users and advocates who actively promote ethical AI practices by equipping young individuals with knowledge about the consequences of AI on privacy, fairness, and social justice (Sitaula et al., 2023).

Furthermore, companies must set up strong governance structures and moral standards for AI research and application, ensuring that moral issues are incorporated into all phases of the AI lifecycle. Corporations may demonstrate their commitment to responsible AI governance and reduce risks related to AI technology by adhering to ethical standards and best practices (Sitaula et al., 2023). In conclusion, companies must interact with young people between 18 and 25 in a transparent, inclusive, and educational manner to address AI's ethical concerns in autonomous systems. Corporations can ensure that AI technologies benefit society while minimizing potential risks and harms by prioritizing transparency, fostering ethical discussions, promoting AI literacy, and implementing robust governance frameworks. It will help to build trust and confidence among young adults and broader stakeholders.

Social Repercussion

Companies need to prioritize social responsibility when integrating AI into autonomous systems. Young people between 18 and 25 are important stakeholders and the generation that will shape society norms and values. First and foremost, businesses must actively participate in candid conversations with young adults to learn about their worries, viewpoints, and goals about AI-driven technology (Rafiq et al., 2022). Companies may ensure that AI's social ramifications are fully considered and handled in their decision-making processes by promoting an inclusive and participatory approach. Organizations should prioritize diversity, equity, and inclusion while developing and implementing AI to reduce possible biases and inequities.

Corporations may cultivate justice, openness, and accountability in designing and deploying AI systems, promoting trust and acceptance among young adults and the greater community. It can be achieved by embracing varied voices and viewpoints. Additionally, businesses ought to fund awareness and education efforts aimed at young adults to foster AI literacy and provide them with the tools necessary to manage the societal ramifications of AI technology successfully (Rafiq et al., 2022). Corporations may enable young adults to advocate for ethical and responsible AI usage in their communities and workplaces by equipping them with the information and critical thinking skills needed to comprehend the social consequences of AI.

Companies should also regularly monitor and assess how AI technologies affect society, getting input from stakeholders and young adults to spot any issues or unexpected repercussions.

Businesses should ensure that their AI projects benefit social well-being and human flourishing by embracing a continuous improvement attitude and modifying their AI strategy in response to changing societal requirements and values (U. Lee et al., 2014).

Overall, companies must interact with young individuals between the ages of 18 and 25 in a transparent, inclusive, and educational manner if they want to address the societal ramifications of AI in autonomous systems. Corporations can ethically and constructively negotiate the social difficulties of AI technology, creating open discourse, diversity, equity, and inclusion and developing trust and confidence among young adults and the greater community.

Business Implications

Businesses must have a favorable public image to attract clients, investors, and top personnel. If they do not deal with the ethical issues surrounding AI, their brand trust and reputation will suffer, costing them sales and market share. Violations of ethics in the application of AI may result in regulatory attention and perhaps legal ramifications. Customers are becoming more conscious of the ethical ramifications of AI, including job displacement, algorithmic prejudice, and data privacy (Robinson, 2019).

Businesses must show their commitment to ethical AI practices and openness in developing and applying AI systems to gain and keep customers' trust.

Staff Morale: Preserving staff morale and productivity also requires addressing ethical considerations related to AI. A corporation that uses AI without considering ethical issues may make employees uncomfortable working there, which might lower job satisfaction and increase attrition. Businesses' capacity to remain viable may be affected in the long run if ethical considerations and societal effects of AI are ignored. To be successful in the long run and remain competitive in the market, one must establish trust among stakeholders and the general public (Robinson, 2019).

Autonomous Systems and SMCR Model

In light of AI and autonomous systems, young adults between the ages of 18 and 25 must redesign Berlo's SMCR communication model. Due to the dynamic nature of communication in the digital era, it is necessary. While still applicable, Berlo's model—which breaks down communication into Source, Message, Channel, and Receiver—needs to be modified to consider the intricacies of AI-driven communication. When it comes to AI, a person may not always be the source of communication (Robinson, 2019). The power of AI algorithms and autonomous systems to create and distribute messages on their own raises concerns about transparency and responsibility.

AI can analyze enormous volumes of data to provide customized messages for each receiver. Nevertheless, this also raises manipulation, privacy, and algorithmic prejudice issues. AI allows communication via chatbots, social media, and virtual assistants, among other channels. Companies must ensure these channels respect user rights and privacy while being safe and easily accessible. The person receiving the communication might be an AI, a human, or both. Young adults must learn how to decipher and assess AI system signals critically, with a particular focus on possible biases and covert intentions.

Remodeling Berlo's SMCR communication model for the digital age necessitates considering factors like accountability, transparency, bias, the changing roles of human and non-human actors in communication processes, and factors like AI and autonomous systems. It is crucial for young adults to successfully and morally negotiate the intricacies of AI-driven communication. Because AI-driven autonomous systems depend on high-quality data for validation, training, and decision-making, organizations are more susceptible to data-related issues, including bias, errors, and data breaches, compromising system dependability and performance (Schwartz et al., 2017).

Ethical and Responsible Use of AI Technologies

Many companies use AI algorithms to find suitable applicants and filter job applications. However, if trained on biased data, these algorithms can potentially reinforce preexisting prejudices in recruiting procedures. For instance, if past hiring data demonstrates a bias against applicants from particular demographics, the AI system may pick up on and perpetuate these biases, unjustly favoring young adults from underrepresented groups between the ages of 18 and 25 (Agarwal et al., 2020).

Much information is gathered by social media platforms on its users, particularly young adults (i.e., between the ages of 18 and 25). AI algorithms for content recommendation and targeted advertising are frequently trained using this data (U. Lee et al., 2014). Nevertheless, improper handling or security breaches of sensitive data may result in identity theft and privacy violations. For example, sensitive information about young adults, including their online conduct, social connections, and personal preferences, may be made public by a social media platform data breach.

To evaluate risk and creditworthiness, financial organizations depend more on AI algorithms. These algorithms could unintentionally bias young people between the ages of 18 and 25 based on characteristics like age, gender, or race, though, if they are not adequately reviewed and controlled. For instance, an AI-driven loan approval system may unjustly refuse loans to young adults from underrepresented areas or with a short credit history, sustaining economic inequality cycles (Schwartz et al., 2017).

Healthcare institutions gather and retain private medical information about young adults (ages 18 to 25). AI systems may be trained with this data to increase the precision of diagnoses and treatment results. However, hacks and data breaches may occur if this data are not sufficiently safeguarded. For example, a compromise in electronic health data may reveal private medical information on young adults, which might result in identity theft and privacy breaches.

Academic institutions gather information about students' behavior, learning preferences, and academic achievement. Predictive analytics tools and personalized learning platforms are two examples of AI-driven educational solutions frequently developed using this data (Schwartz et al., 2017). However, if this information is misapplied or construed, it may result in young adults between 18 and 25 being mistreated and facing prejudice in the classroom. For instance, a grading system powered by AI may penalize pupils for things like learning difficulties or socioeconomic status outside their control (U. Lee et al., 2014).

In each case, young adults between 18 and 25 might be disproportionately impacted by data-related problems with AI-driven autonomous systems, either through discrimination, privacy infringement, or biased decision-making. Businesses must address these concerns to guarantee AI technology's moral and responsible application. Overall, while AI-driven autonomous systems provide enormous commercial prospects, young adults must carefully weigh the dangers and difficulties involved to ensure effective deployment and long-term growth in the quickly changing field of autonomous technology (Sitaula et al., 2023).

Recommendation Systems

Employ user behavior and preferences to recommend goods, services, or content. Some examples include personalized suggestions on social networking, e-commerce websites, and streaming platforms. Businesses may increase customer loyalty and retention by providing tailored suggestions. Customers are more likely to return to platforms that recognize and appropriately accommodate their preferences (Basu et al., 2023). From a commercial standpoint, recommendation systems powered by AI have several benefits and drawbacks for young adults (Batool & Yosuf, 2023). AI recommendation systems offer customized recommendations based on the user's tastes, resulting in a more enjoyable and engaging user experience across platforms, applications, and websites.

By offering appropriate goods or services to consumers based on their behavior, personalized suggestions may help businesses increase sales and income. It can result in improved conversion rates and happier customers. Through analyzing user data and behavior, AI recommendation systems help firms focus their marketing efforts more precisely by identifying potential consumers and delivering appropriate promotional messages or advertising (Batool & Yosuf, 2023). AI recommendation systems enable young adults to make data-driven decisions in product development, marketing tactics, and company operations by offering insightful information on user preferences, trends, and behavior.

Customized Recommendations

Online apparel merchants frequently use AI recommendation algorithms to promote clothes, accessories, and styles that suit young adults' fashion tastes. The recommendation algorithm can promote fashionable products like graphic shirts, shoes, or denim jackets to a young adult who regularly peruses casual streetwear brands or follows fashion influencers on social media. Netflix, Hulu, and Spotify use AI algorithms to suggest movies, TV series, and songs to young adult consumers based on their viewing and listening preferences (Schwartz et al., 2017). For instance, a young adult's enjoyment of sci-fi movies or indie rock music may be enhanced by the recommendation system's suggestions for appropriate films or playlists with related material.

AI recommendation algorithms are used by video game platforms like Steam and PlayStation Network to select titles that fit the interests and gaming preferences of young adults. The recommendation algorithm may provide well-liked games in genres like action-adventure or multiplayer shooters (e.g., if a young adult loves playing those games; Batool & Yosuf, 2023). It increases the possibility of finding new and exciting games to play. Based on their young adult customers' dietary restrictions and gastronomic tastes, meal delivery apps such as DoorDash and Uber Eats utilize AI recommendation algorithms to offer restaurants and food alternatives.

For example, the recommendation system can highlight local restaurants that serve plant-based alternatives or popular dishes within those categories if a young adult often eats vegetarian or vegan meals. AI recommendation algorithms are used by social networking platforms like Instagram and TikTok to propose material, profiles, and hashtags that suit the interests and preferences of young adult users (Batool & Yosuf, 2023). For example, suppose a young adult interacts with material about travel and adventure or follows accounts about health and well-being. In that case, the recommendation algorithm may customize their feed with influencers and articles that are comparable to theirs, improving their social media experience.

These examples demonstrate how AI recommendation systems employ user data and behavioral patterns to provide tailored recommendations that appeal to the interests and preferences of young adults between the ages of 18 and 25. Businesses may boost customer happiness, grow sales, and enhance engagement with this demographic category by providing pertinent goods, services, and information (Batool & Yosuf, 2023).

Competitive Advantage

Companies may obtain a competitive advantage by providing superior tailored experiences, drawing in and keeping consumers, and successfully boosting brand loyalty by utilizing AI recommendation systems. Because AI recommendation systems rely on gathering and evaluating user data, privacy, data protection, and the possible abuse of personal data are raised (Caulley et al., 2023). It can erode user confidence and draw attention from regulators. Recommendation algorithms may unintentionally reinforce biases seen in the training set, producing unfair or discriminating suggestions based on racial, gender, or socioeconomic status. Such recommendations can harm a company's reputation and put it in legal trouble.

Companies risk becoming too dependent on AI recommendation systems, ignoring human judgment and intuition in making decisions (Chu et al., 2023). It might lead to lost opportunities, subpar user experiences, and decreased creativity. Personalized suggestions can produce "filter bubbles," in which consumers are only exposed to goods or information that confirms their preexisting opinions. It can reduce the diversity of viewpoints and even lead to the polarization or echo chambers that confident young adults have in society. AI recommendation systems give preference to information or items that consumers have already interacted with, which can stifle creativity and exploration by limiting the chance of unexpectedly discovering novel concepts, goods, or experiences (Bae et al., 2023).

Developing and sustaining AI recommendation systems' technical difficulties include algorithm selection, data processing, model training, and optimization. These tasks require specialized knowledge and resources, which may be difficult for young adults and startups to get and manage (Ehrlén et al., 2023). In conclusion, even though AI recommendation systems have a lot to offer companies, young adults need to be aware of the risks and challenges that come with them, like bias, privacy issues, and excessive reliance on algorithms, to ensure that their business strategies are implemented responsibly and successfully.

Predictive Analytics

Organizations can foresee trends, spot patterns, and make data-driven choices using AI for predictive modeling and analytics. It is helpful in industries including marketing, healthcare, and finance (Caulley et al., 2023). Thanks to AI-powered predictive modeling, which improves resource allocation and strategic planning, young adults may make data-driven decisions based on precise projections and insights. Businesses that use AI for predictive analytics get a competitive advantage by seeing new trends, gauging client demands, and making proactive strategy adjustments to stay one step ahead of rivals. By automating data analysis procedures, AI frees up young adults' time and energy to evaluate findings and draw practical conclusions to propel corporate expansion.

Customer Loyalty

Young adults may improve customer happiness and loyalty by using predictive analytics to personalize customer interactions, anticipate preferences, and customize products or services to match individual needs (Ebeling & Gebhard, 2022). AI-powered predictive modeling helps young adults minimize risks like market swings, supply chain interruptions, and financial losses while optimizing prospects for growth and profitability by anticipating future hazards and opportunities. By spotting market gaps, new trends, and consumer wants, predictive analytics encourages creativity and gives young adults the tools they need to create new goods, services, and business models that adapt to the changing requirements and tastes of the market.

High-Quality Data

High-quality data are necessary for predictive analytics to produce effective modeling and analysis, but young adults may face problems with incomplete, erroneous, or biased data, which can produce forecasts that are not trustworthy and lead to poor decision-making. Large-scale data collection and analysis for predictive modeling creates privacy difficulties, especially regarding using sensitive or personal data (Fein et al., 2007). It can damage stakeholder and consumer confidence and cause problems with regulatory compliance. AI-powered predictive analytics implementation necessitates specific technical knowledge in ML, data science, and programming, which might be difficult for young people without these resources or abilities to master.

Young adults may find it challenging to comprehend and elucidate the underlying causes driving forecasts when using AI models, such as neural networks, for predictive analytics. It might erode their trust and confidence in the model's outputs (Islam et al., 2024). Predictive analytics that largely depends on AI has the risk of inducing technological dependence and exposing companies to risks, including algorithmic biases, data breaches, and system failures that can ruin their brand and disrupt corporate operations. It may be expensive to develop and implement AI-powered predictive analytics solutions. These solutions require expenditures in technological infrastructure, personnel acquisition, data collecting, and continuous maintenance. Young adults and startups may find it difficult to finance these costs.

Although young business adults can benefit significantly from AI-powered predictive analytics, some risks and challenges must be addressed to ensure successful implementation and maximize the value of predictive modeling in fostering business success (Straand et al., 2024).

These risks and challenges include data quality issues, privacy concerns, and technical complexity.

Robotics

AI-powered robotics incorporate AI algorithms into robotic systems, allowing them to see their environment, decide for themselves, and carry out tasks without human intervention. AI in robotics opens new employment paths for young adults in programming, maintenance, robotics engineering, and supervision (Hilty et al., 2023). Young individuals may improve their employability in the future job market by working with AI-powered robotics to gain valuable skills in programming, data analysis, problem-solving, and robotics technology. Robotics driven by AI may automate tedious processes, boosting corporate productivity and efficiency. It can provide businesses using such technology with cost savings and competitive benefits.

Engaging in AI-Powered Robotics

Engaging with AI-powered robotics helps young adults address complicated challenges via creativity and invention, which promotes an innovative culture in enterprises. Businesses may get a competitive edge in their respective sectors by using AI-powered robots early on. It will enable them to remain ahead of their competition and satisfy changing customer needs (He et al., 2022). AI-driven robotics can replace some occupations, especially those requiring repetitive or physical labor.

Young people lacking the ability to move into new occupations might lead to underemployment or unemployment. Specialized skills are needed to use AI-powered robots, and there can be a disconnect between what young adults now have and what employers need (Batool & Yosuf, 2023). It can make it more difficult for them to take advantage of employment chances in this industry.

Businesses must budget significantly for equipment procurement, deployment, and training when investing in AI-powered robotics. Young adults' employment options may be limited because this cost load discourages some organizations from implementing this technology (Batool & Yosuf, 2023). Robotics driven by AI brings up moral and societal issues such as data privacy, employment displacement, and the abuse of AI technology. Young adults in this sector could have to deal with moral conundrums and face public scrutiny.

Businesses that rely too heavily on AI-powered robotics may be more susceptible to cyberattacks, technical malfunctions, and other technological hazards. It could be necessary for young adults to create backup plans and procedures to reduce these hazards (Ashton et al., 2023). In summary, although AI-driven robotics provide many advantages for companies and youth, some drawbacks must be resolved to guarantee a good effect on the labor force and society.

Virtual Assistants

Siri, Google Assistant, and Amazon Alexa employ ML and NLP to comprehend and reply to user inquiries, carry out tasks, and deliver information. From a commercial standpoint, young adults may benefit from and be disadvantageous to using AI-powered virtual assistants. Virtual assistants may handle mundane duties like email management, appointment scheduling, and information provision, freeing young adults to concentrate on higher-value and more strategically oriented work (Behizadeh et al., 2023). Virtual assistants help young adults save time by automating monotonous chores, allowing them to work more effectively and productively.

Impacts of Virtual Assistants

Virtual assistants may help young adults with chores anytime, anywhere, and are available around the clock, which improves flexibility and convenience in the workplace

(Behizadeh et al., 2023). Without hiring more employees, virtual assistants may grow their help in response to demand, meeting changes in workload and business requirements (Ashton et al., 2023). Virtual assistants may save organizations money by lowering the need for more administrative workers or making costly office infrastructure investments (Boustani et al., 2022). Excessive dependence on virtual assistants may result in technological dependency and a decline in young adults' problem-solving and decision-making abilities. Virtual assistants can misunderstand complicated questions or linguistic subtleties, which might result in communication problems (P. Lee et al., 2022).

Virtual assistants might be exposed to cybersecurity concerns, including hacking or data breaches, which could endanger private information belonging to young adults and critical company data. Virtual assistants may cause some administrative jobs often filled by young adults to become obsolete, which might mean losing your job or having to retrain for a different position (Behizadeh et al., 2023). Young adults in business may get several advantages from AI-powered virtual assistants, such as enhanced productivity, time savings, and scalability. To optimize their efficacy and reduce hazards, they also bring obstacles like privacy issues, reliance on technology, and the possibility of job displacement. These issues must be adequately controlled by using the SMCR communication remodel.

Exploring Berlo's SMCR Communication Model

Berlo's SMCR communication model is a vital component that is the foundation for our investigation (Ghoreishi, 2023). Given that it has long been a pillar of communication theory, it is essential to comprehend its history, complexities, and constraints. The review will give a thorough summary of the main ideas and components of the model, which has served as a framework for decades in the study of communication. Businesses may create more focused and efficient communication strategies by learning about young adults' preferences, actions, and preferred communication channels (Behizadeh et al., 2023). It may result in higher levels of engagement, brand loyalty, and consumer satisfaction among this group.

By modifying Berlo's approach to AI-driven communication, companies may better target and customize their marketing efforts toward young adults. Increased conversion rates and a higher return on investment for marketing campaigns may come from this. Businesses may strengthen their relationships with young adults (18 to 25 years old) and encourage brand advocacy and loyalty by customizing their communication methods to appeal to this group. Comprehending how young adults view and engage with AI-powered communication may assist companies in forging more profound and genuine bonds with their intended demographic (Behizadeh et al., 2023).

Young Adults and Communication

Young adults increasingly use AI-powered devices, platforms, and apps (Baldauf et al., 2021). Therefore, understanding how this technology affects their development and well-being is essential. The research study examined AI-powered technology's excellent and adverse effects on young adults. Young individuals between 18 and 25 are among the first to use AI-powered gadgets, platforms, and applications. It is possible to gain insight into how AI technology affects young adults' routines, behaviors, and decision-making processes by analyzing their adoption and usage patterns (Baldauf et al., 2021). Young adulthood is a crucial period of growth marked by self-discovery, identity-building, and the move toward independence.

How AI-powered technology affects young adults' cognitive, social, and emotional development during this time can significantly influence their future paths and general well-being. Berlo’s SMCR communication model is a crucial element forming our inquiry.

Understanding its background, intricacies, and limitations is crucial since communication theory has relied on it for a considerable time. The study provides a comprehensive overview of the key concepts and elements of the model, which has been used as a framework for communication research for many years. Its communication model has far-reaching consequences beyond theoretical communication studies (Bhat et al., 2023). The way businesses engage and connect with young adults in the current business environment has a significant influence on how successful they are.

A Commercial Perspective

The research delved into applying the communication remodel from a commercial perspective, emphasizing its importance in comprehending and interacting with the young adult customer base (Boustani et al., 2022). The evaluation considers AI-powered technology's significant effects on young adults' growth and well-being as their connection with it changes. It evaluates critically if a new communication model is necessary to capture the intricate communication patterns of the digital era.

The study's nature and methodology are covered in more detail in the following parts, guaranteeing a thorough and knowledgeable investigation of the interconnected aspects of young adults, AI-powered technologies, communication models, and their future consequences (Straand et al., 2024). The research lays the groundwork for thoroughly investigating the dynamic connection between young adults and AI-powered technology and its significant effects on development, communication, and well-being while keeping these fundamental ideas in mind.

The researcher's primary focus was exploring the future implications of AI-powered technology for young adults, with the overarching objective of establishing a revised communication model (Cox, 2021). Current trends and research aim in this context. It is crucial to consider how young adults' behavior may evolve and the potential positive and negative impacts that may arise, with a concerted effort to mitigate any adverse consequences associated with smart device usage.

The research study was structured around three key areas, each contributing to comprehending the imperative for a revised communication model. First and foremost, it is essential to explain the term 'young adult' in the context of this research. As mentioned in Chapter One, the demographic encompasses individuals aged 18 to 25 and coming of age in an era where modern technology and intelligent electronic devices are ubiquitous (Mollborn et al., 2021). Within this demographic, the prevalence of AI-powered devices is striking. Young adults frequently acquire such devices for various purposes, including communication, education, and entertainment (Baldauf et al., 2021).

Notably, they exhibit a higher level of digital competence and adaptability than other generations, often initiating their interaction with AI-powered electronic devices at an early age and swiftly becoming proficient in utilizing technology (Akyol, 2023). The anticipated repercussions of AI-powered technology on young adults underscore the urgent need for a fresh communication paradigm considering the evolving technological landscape. Several critical factors and potential implications underscore this shift. One salient aspect is AI's ever-improving ability to customize information, products, and services tailored to millennials (T. Chen, 2022). However, this personalization risks reinforcing filter bubbles, potentially constraining exposure to diverse viewpoints and fostering highly individualized experiences.

The Increasing Integration of AI Systems

Furthermore, the increasing integration of AI systems into decision-making processes raises concerns about algorithmic bias, which could manifest in prejudiced outcomes for young adults, such as biased algorithms influencing college admissions, loan approvals, and job applications (Chan et al., 2022). Consequently, the widespread utilization of AI necessitates robust data protection measures to safeguard against such issues. It is imperative to recognize that AI-powered tools, including chatbots, voice assistants, and social media algorithms, have the potential to reshape how young adults engage in communication (Baldauf et al., 2021). Thus, any updated communication model must account for AI's dual role as both a source and a recipient within the communication process.

The research effort delved into the profound implications of AI-powered technology on the young adult demographic, highlighting the imperative for a revised communication model. By assessing current trends and research findings, the study elucidated the anticipated transformations in youth behavior over the next decade, primarily driven by the increasing prevalence of intelligent electronic devices (Caulley et al., 2023).

Its investigation is structured around three key focal points, encompassing the identification of potential obstacles, stimulating interventions and strategies, and promoting overall well-being and positive development among young adults. As we venture further into the AI-dominated landscape, we should adopt the SMCR communication remodel to effectively navigate the evolving technological terrain and its implications for the younger generation.

Impacts on Young Adults' Overall Wellbeing and Business

Another critical aspect to consider is the potential impact on young adults' mental health and overall well-being resulting from the increasing utilization of AI-powered social media and entertainment platforms (Chan et al., 2022). User engagement metrics are frequently used by businesses running AI-powered social media and entertainment platforms to gauge their performance.

However, excessive use of these platforms can lead to detrimental effects on young adults' mental health, including social isolation, despair, and anxiety (Baldauf et al., 2021). Companies have to strike a balance between the requirement to put consumers' mental health first and the objective of optimizing user engagement. The reputation and dependability of the companies that operate AI-powered social media and entertainment platforms may be impacted by how these platforms influence the mental health of young adults.

User trust can be undermined, and a brand's reputation can be damaged by unfavorable opinions or public outcry over mental health concerns (Deshmukh, 2021). It might result in a decline in users and income. Companies using AI-powered platforms must abide by legal and regulatory standards about consumer protection, data security, and user privacy. If mental health issues resulting from platform use are not addressed, firms may be subject to legal risks like litigation, penalties, and regulatory enforcement measures. Businesses are under growing pressure to show their commitment to corporate social responsibility (CSR) by tackling societal concerns and improving the lives of their consumers and communities as awareness of mental health issues rises (Deshmukh, 2021).

Creating programs and materials to assist the mental health and general well-being of young adults may improve a business's image for corporate social responsibility and cultivate goodwill among stakeholders (Deshmukh, 2021). Addressing cyberbullying and addictive behaviors will be paramount in mitigating any adverse effects. Furthermore, it is imperative to incorporate the influence of AI on professional and educational advancement into the new communication model to counteract any detrimental consequences associated with the overuse of AI devices within the working population. An essential component of this strategy involves promoting digital literacy among young adults, equipping them with the necessary tools to responsibly engage with AI-powered technology and critically assess AI-generated information (T. Chen, 2022).

Pre- Post Pandemic Impacts on Young Adults to Business

The other vital factor is the pandemic and how the pre-pandemic and post-pandemic affected young adults' lives. Several patterns in schooling exist before, during, and after the pandemic. Before the pandemic, conventional classroom instruction, standardized testing, and restricted technology usage (Deshmukh, 2021). During the pandemic, remote and online learning gained popularity quickly, young adults relied more on technology, flexible and adaptable teaching techniques were prioritized, and the value of social and emotional learning was realized (Deshmukh, 2021). Following the pandemic, education may shift toward a hybrid model that combines face-to-face and virtual instruction, ongoing technological integration, a greater emphasis on tailored and comprehensive instruction, and a greater understanding of the significance of mental health and well-being (Liu et al., 2022).

Minimizing Negative Impacts

Ethical considerations must come to the forefront of AI development to minimize the negative impact (Deshmukh, 2021). The overarching objective should be creating and utilizing AI that does not harm young adults (Korol & Bevelander, 2021). Thus, ethical issues should be integrated as a central element within the updated communication model. Another pertinent concern pertains to technological dependence, where the increasing reliance on AI for various tasks may lead to potential over-dependence on technology, potentially diminishing young adult's ability to solve problems independently without the assistance of AI (Chan et al., 2022). It is imperative to enhance cybersecurity measures within the new communication model while implementing comprehensive regulations to protect young adults' rights, privacy, and overall well-being in AI-powered technology (Deshmukh, 2021).

A redesigned communication model should unequivocally recognize AI as a pivotal component of communication, considering the multifaceted consequences it entails (Deshmukh, 2021). Its holistic approach should encompass an assessment of the potential advantages and challenges associated with AI-powered technology, advocate for ethical AI development, prioritize privacy concerns, and empower young adults with the knowledge and skills needed to navigate the AI-driven world effectively (Liu et al., 2022). To further empower young adults in the age of AI, fostering multidisciplinary collaboration between young adults, technological experts, educators, legislators, and psychologists will be indispensable (T. Chen, 2022). Consequently, it is imperative first to elucidate the benefits of AI-powered technology to underscore the significance of such collaborative efforts (Liu et al., 2022).

Young Adult Empowerment

Businesses may benefit significantly from the empowerment of young individuals (18 to 25 years old) who grew up with technology at their fingertips thanks to AI-powered gadgets. Businesses have chances to understand better, engage, and service the young adult audience due to their empowerment through AI-powered products. Organizations may remain relevant and competitive in an increasingly digital and connected world by utilizing AI technology in marketing, product creation, consumer interaction, and education.

Harnessing the Advantages

AI-driven apps and platforms can personalize information, suggestions, and user experiences based on individual tastes and behaviors, as noted by Sixto-García and Duarte Melo (2020). Its personalization fosters a sense of engagement and connection among young adults, enhancing the relevance of information and services. Additionally, AI contributes to time efficiency by automating various tasks and processes, saving young adults valuable time in their daily lives. Young adults can redirect their focus toward other essential responsibilities thanks to virtual assistants, AI-driven scheduling applications, and predictive text capabilities (Sixto-García & Duarte Melo, 2020).

Young individuals now enjoy swift and effortless access to knowledge courtesy of AI-powered search engines and information retrieval systems, as observed by Jiménez Correa et al. (2021). Accessibility empowers individuals to expand their knowledge, stay informed about current events, and obtain instant answers to their questions through voice assistants and chatbots, encouraging face-to-face interactions and reducing communication barriers (Ashton et al., 2023). Moreover, at the same time, AI-driven games, music, and art applications open doors to creative and innovative pursuits, contributing to maximizing their benefits through redesign.

AI positively impacts young adults' health and well-being (Ashton et al., 2023). AI-powered health applications enable them to monitor their physical and emotional well-being, keeping tabs on their exercise routines, sleep patterns, and potential health risks. AI-driven smart home systems and appliances enhance comfort and convenience, offering features like energy management, voice-controlled home automation, and heightened security (Ashton et al., 2023). Additionally, AI-driven devices create new professional opportunities for young adults, particularly in fields such as data science, AI development, and ML, potentially giving them a competitive edge in the job market (Ashton et al., 2023).

Business Limitations

Even though the SMCR communication model has long been used as a fundamental framework for comprehending commercial communication operations, its use has several problems in today's dynamic, digitally driven environment. Since new communication channels like social media, online forums, and instant messaging platforms are interactive, the old SMCR model ignores their interactive character and instead assumes a linear flow of communication from the sender to the recipient. In the current digital environment, communication is frequently bidirectional, with real-time interactions and feedback loops influencing the transmission and interpretation of messages (Tropschuh et al., 2022).

The SMCR model gives feedback mechanisms with little weight, which makes it difficult for firms to evaluate the success of their communication campaigns and make necessary adjustments. Businesses use feedback measures like engagement rates, click-through rates, and sentiment analysis in today's data-driven environment to determine audience response and improve their messaging (Tropschuh et al., 2022). The SMCR model oversimplifies communication by emphasizing message transmission from sender to recipient while ignoring the impact of contextual elements such as social dynamics, technical platforms, and cultural norms. Businesses need to ensure that messages are relevant, resonate, and effective by considering the specific environment in which they are communicated (Tropschuh et al., 2022).

Businesses must deal with the issue of channel fragmentation, which occurs when their target audience is spread across several online and offline channels due to the growth of digital communication platforms and channels. The conventional SMCR model does not consider this fragmentation, which results in inefficient channel selection and resource allocation during communication operations. The ethical issues surrounding communication methods, such as privacy, openness, and authenticity, are not explicitly considered by the SMCR model (Tropschuh et al., 2022). Businesses must prioritize ethical communication practices of increased responsibility and scrutiny to gain their stakeholders' confidence and trust. Because the SMCR model was created before the advent of digital platforms, it can be challenging to keep up with the quick changes in communication technology.

With the advantages of cutting-edge technologies like chatbots, virtual reality, and AI, businesses must constantly modify their communication strategy (Tropschuh et al., 2022). These technologies may not fit cleanly into the conventional SMCR framework. The SMCR communication model offers a basic knowledge of communication processes, but there are many obstacles to overcome in the modern corporate environment because of interaction, feedback, context, channel fragmentation, ethical issues, and technology improvements. In the digital age, businesses must be aware of these constraints and implement more flexible and subtle communication strategies to interact with their stakeholders (Tropschuh et al., 2022).

Enhancing Mobility

AI technology also plays a crucial role in enhancing mobility for young adults with impairments, promoting inclusivity and equal opportunities through assistive devices that aid in communication, mobility, and access to digital content (Ghoreishi, 2023). Moreover, AI-powered decision-support solutions assist young adults in making informed choices, offering data-driven insights for improved decision-making in areas ranging from financial planning to educational options. Language learning experiences are also enhanced through AI language learning platforms, which tailor exercises and courses based on individual progress and preferences, thereby increasing the effectiveness and personalization of language acquisition (Ghoreishi, 2023).

Environmental Concerns

In addition to its various benefits, AI contributes positively to environmental concerns. AI can optimize resource utilization, encourage sustainable behaviors, and reduce carbon footprints, enabling young adults to contribute actively to a greener future (Ghoreishi, 2023). Overall, AI-powered technologies significantly augment young adults' future potential. As AI technology continues to evolve and adapt to their ever-changing needs, we can anticipate even more substantial advancements in education, employment opportunities, healthcare, and daily life.

By embracing AI, young adults are poised to embark on a more connected, creative, and productive future, fostering a sense of community and collaboration that will propel them forward in the fast-paced digital world. The limitless opportunities offered by AI position young adults to reap significant rewards as technology continues to play an increasingly pivotal role in reshaping our environment (Ghoreishi, 2023).

Significant energy and computing resources are needed to develop and implement AI technologies, which harm the environment by increasing carbon emissions and electronic waste (Ghoreishi, 2023). Concerns over the sustainability of AI infrastructure and its impact on climate change are intensifying as AI use grows. AI powered decision-making systems may raise moral questions about justice, accountability, and transparency. In environmental management, for example, automated decision-making procedures may unintentionally give preference to some interests or results over others, resulting in unforeseen repercussions or moral conundrums (Ghoreishi, 2023).

Young adults' capacity to engage in and impact environmental governance may be restricted if AI technologies are widely used in environmental decision-making processes. It might reduce human autonomy and agency. Outsourcing decision-making authority to AI systems raises concerns because it may marginalize human viewpoints and values in environmental planning and policy (Ghoreishi, 2023). These worries highlight the importance of including ethical issues, transparency, and stakeholder participation in AI-powered environmental projects within an SMCR communication remodel framework. Companies and organizations must aggressively seek feedback and input from various stakeholders, including young adults while being upfront and transparent about AI technology's possible hazards and limits (Ghoreishi, 2023).

Impact of AI-Powered Technology on Young Adults

Young individuals between 18 and 25 are significantly impacted by AI-powered technology, which presents potential and concerns (Gaftandzhieva et al., 2023). To effectively interact with young adults in today's fast-expanding digital ecosystem, a more dynamic and adaptable communication strategy is necessary, one of the significant business issues that has been recognized. The pre-digital SMCR communication paradigm may not sufficiently address the complexity and subtleties of communication in the contemporary corporate environment.

The standard SMCR model ignores the interactive and multidirectional character of communication channels like social media, instant messaging, and online forums, which assumes a linear flow of communication from sender to receiver through a preset channel (Gaftandzhieva et al., 2023). As digital natives, young adults between 18 and 25 are used to collaborating on content creation, exchanging comments, and having real-time conversations on various digital platforms. As a result, companies need to embrace a more adaptable and dynamic communication strategy that considers how dynamic digital communication is (Gaftandzhieva et al., 2023).

Exploring Consequences

Young adults stand to reap significant benefits from AI-powered technology, but carefully examining and addressing its potential drawbacks is equally crucial. These consequences encompass several vital aspects. In their quest to tailor interactions, AI systems often amass and scrutinize vast quantities of user data, raising concerns among young adults about the extent of personal information collected and employed by AI algorithms, thereby triggering privacy issues (C. Kang et al., 2023).

AI-driven content curation, while offering personalized experiences, can inadvertently lead to the creation of filter bubbles. These bubbles confine young adults to a limited spectrum of content that reinforces their existing viewpoints, potentially culminating in echo chambers where diverse perspectives and critical thinking are stifled (C. Kang et al., 2023). Furthermore, algorithmic bias poses another challenge, with AI algorithms susceptible to inadvertently perpetuating biases in their training data. The implications of such biases, ranging from biased loan approvals to college admissions and job applications, can potentially impact young adults' opportunities and experiences (Tropschuh et al., 2022).

The continuous connectivity and exposure to social media, facilitated by AI-driven content recommendations, can also have detrimental effects on young adults' mental health, contributing to heightened levels of anxiety, depression, and feelings of inadequacy (Tropschuh et al., 2022). Moreover, an excessive reliance on AI-driven communication channels may hinder the development of critical social skills, fostering feelings of isolation and detachment. Over-reliance on AI solutions can lead to a diminishing capacity for critical thinking and self-reliance as young adults age (Gaftandzhieva et al., 2023).

Using screens before bed or during the night can interfere with sleep cycles, making it harder to fall asleep and get enough restful sleep (Kaniasty, 2012). The blue light that screens generate has the potential to disrupt sleep patterns and increase weariness by interfering with the hormone melatonin's ability to regulate sleep cycles. Screen time in excess can harm a person's ability to communicate and engage with others in social situations. These young adults may spend less time interacting in person, creating bonds with others, and learning necessary social skills like empathy, active listening, and nonverbal communication.

Privacy and Safety Concerns

The specter of job disruption looms as AI automation advances, potentially displacing workers and leaving young adults anxious about the future of their career prospects. Integrating AI into various applications opens new avenues for cyberattacks and data breaches, jeopardizing young adults' privacy and online safety. AI-generated content can be weaponized to spread misinformation, posing a significant societal threat (Heller, 2012). Ethical dilemmas surrounding AI development and deployment, such as the moral implications of AI in autonomous vehicles or weaponry systems, further complicate the landscape. Moreover, the risk of technological dependence looms large, with young adults potentially becoming overly reliant on AI for various tasks at the cost of traditional skills and expertise.

Balanced Approach

A balanced approach that acknowledges the advantages of AI while minimizing its potential hazards is essential in addressing these multifaceted issues. Collaboration among policymakers, educators, technology developers, and society is imperative to ensure that AI-powered technology positively influences young adults' lives, safeguarding their well-being and privacy. It entails the establishment of ethical standards, increased transparency in data handling, and promotion of digital literacy as essential components of this collective effort (Heller, 2012).

Berlo's SMCR Communication Model

American communication theorist K. Berlo created the SMCR model, published in the year 1960 in 'The Process of Communication: An Introduction to Theory and Practice' (Berlo,

1960). The model developed by David K. Berlo, a well-known pioneer in communication studies, has become the cornerstone for researching and comprehending the communication process. The model was developed to conceptualize and delineate. To study and enhance communication in various circumstances, including interpersonal, organizational, and mass communication, Berlo set out to develop a framework.

The SMCR model is a helpful resource for academics, educators, and practitioners in communication due to its clarity and simplicity (Chin et al., 2024). It has inspired later communication theories and models and has been frequently taught and cited in communication studies. The SMCR model continues to be a proper starting place for comprehending the fundamental elements of communication and how to interact to promote effective communication, even though it has been criticized and improved upon throughout time by various communication academics.

Overview

David K. Berlo created the SMCR communication theory model in 1960. The model is intended to describe the components of effective communication and the communication process itself (Berlo, 1960). The model has four essential parts. In his concept, he emphasizes how crucial it is for the sender and receiver to communicate well throughout the communication process. The SMCR model, which stands for source, message, channel, and receiver, offers a framework for comprehending the processes involved in efficient communication. The SMCR model states that effective communication happens when the sender is educated about the subject matter, communicates clearly and succinctly, chooses the best channel to convey the information, and considers the receiver's requirements and preferences.

The model emphasizes the significance of each component in the communication process and stresses the demand for an engaging, clear, compelling message. The SMCR model has been extensively utilized in various disciplines, including communication studies, education, and business. It has been developed and adjusted to accommodate advancements in communication technology and the changing demands of contemporary audiences and learners. Source, Message, Channel, and Receiver—the four essential elements of every communication process—are the acronym for the SMCR paradigm. Together, these elements support information communication between young adults or groups.

The source is the party or thing that starts the communication process (Heller, 2012). It is in charge of encrypting the information it wants to express because it is the message sender. Communication efficiency is greatly influenced by the source's communication abilities, knowledge, attitudes, and other variables (Baldauf et al., 2021). The message is the information, concept, or material the source wants to get to the recipient. It could be non-verbal, textual, visual, or vocal. The message must be written so the recipient can comprehend and correctly interpret it. The channel is the mechanism or medium to transfer a message from its source to its recipient. Face-to-face interactions, textual correspondence, emails, phone calls, video conferencing, and more can be used as channels. The chosen channel can considerably impact communication clarity and efficiency (Heller, 2012).

The recipient, or group for whom the message is meant, is the receiver that oversees deciphering and analyzing the message transmitted by the source. The recipient's background, knowledge, attitudes, and communication abilities all impact how they interpret and react to the message. Along with these four components, Berlo's SMCR communication model approach acknowledges the significance of noise and feedback in communication: Feedback is the recipient's response or emotional response that was sent. It gives the sender the chance to determine whether the message was received as intended and gives them the chance to clarify or change it as needed.

A feedback loop is typically Any obstruction or interruption that can prevent communication, referred to as noise. Internal and external noise can impair the proper transmission and reception of information. Internal noise includes prejudices and linguistic obstacles. Berlo's SMCR communication model highlights the intricacy of ensuring that messages are sent adequately from one party to another, a valuable framework for studying communication dynamics. It highlights the necessity for transparent encoding and decoding, suitable channels, and constant feedback to improve communication efficacy.

Revisiting the SMCR Model

A conceptual framework that offers an organized manner to comprehend the fundamental elements of communication is the SMCR (Source, Message, Channel, Receiver) model of communication. The communication environment has changed substantially with the arrival of AI-powered technology and the shifting habits of young adults, even though it continues to be essential and effective in many circumstances (Bhat et al., 2023). In the current digital era, the SMCR model may need to be modified or supplemented for the following reasons.

The old idea of channel has changed due to the rise of digital communication channels, including social media, instant messaging applications, and video conferencing. Young adults quickly flip between multiple channels since they have different features and affordances (Bhat et al., 2023). A more subtle approach is necessary to comprehend how these channels affect communication. Digital-era feedback loops have the potential to be quicker and more dynamic. Online real-time chats between young adults are typical, and they frequently get quick feedback.

Its quick input may impact how messages are developed and modified throughout the communication process, which the SMCR model may not fully handle.

Message Personalization and Adaptation

AI-based technologies like chatbots and recommendation engines can customize and modify messages depending on specific user information. Its level of message customization and adaptation may considerably impact communication efficiency. Hence, it must be considered in modern communication models (Bhat et al., 2023). Young adults frequently feel information overload due to the abundance of online information that requires the ability to handle, filter, and critically assess the information they come across. The SMCR model does not directly address this element of information consumption.

The characterization of digital communication is based on interactive and participatory communication. Beyond the linear sender-receiver model in SMCR, young adults participate in two-way and multi-way dialogues, co-creation of material, and social interactions online. Digital communication frequently uses visual and non-verbal features, such as emojis, GIFs, and memes, which give communication additional levels of meaning and emotion (Bhat et al., 2023). The conventional SMCR model might not effectively address these issues. Young adults are increasingly worried about privacy and security in the digital world. Communication models should consider how these issues affect information sharing and trust (Bhat et al., 2023).

The SMCR model offers a basic knowledge of communication, but it can also require the addition of more recent models or frameworks tailored to the intricacies and subtleties of communication in the digital era. Approaches that consider modern communication's dynamic and participatory character include models like the Transactional Model of Communication and the Networked Communication Model. The potential and difficulties provided by young adults' current use of AI-powered technology may be better negotiated by educators, researchers, and practitioners with the aid of adaptations and new models (Bhat et al., 2023).

Urgency for Change

Young adults between 18 and 25 frequently struggle with information overload due to the extensive internet ecosystem in the modern work environment (Bhat et al., 2023). Its deluge demands the capacity to manage, screen, and critically evaluate the vast volumes of data encountered. The SMCR (Sender-Message-Channel-Receiver) model and other conventional communication models offer a basic knowledge of communication processes, but they frequently fail to handle the complexity of information consumption in the digital age.

Digital communication transcends the linear sender-receiver paradigm of the SMCR model with its interactive and participative dynamics (Bhat et al., 2023). Young individuals actively participate in online social interactions, co-create material, and have two-way and multi-way conversations. Furthermore, the widespread use of visual and nonverbal cues like memes, GIFs, and emoticons gives communication subtle meaning and emotion. Conventional communication models could find it difficult to consider these subtleties. The digital sphere is fraught with privacy and security issues, further complicating the communication dynamics for young adults.

The existing SMCR communication model must change to address how the identified problems affect information sharing and foster stakeholder trust. The SMCR model is still a helpful foundation, but it must be supplemented by more modern models suited to the complexities of digital communication. A more sophisticated view of interactions in the digital age is possible because of models like the 'Transactional Model of Communication' and the

'Networked Communication Model,' which shed light on the dynamic and interactive aspects of modern communication (Terzopoulos & Satratzemi, 2020).

To manage the opportunities and difficulties presented by the developments, educators, researchers, and practitioners must adapt and create new communication models, given the growing integration of AI-powered technology into everyday life. Businesses may improve their communication methods and effectively interact with young adults in the digital age by adopting these modifications and utilizing creative frameworks (Bhat et al., 2023).

Comprehensive Strategy

A comprehensive strategy is essential to create an effective redesigned communication model that addresses the challenges and barriers posed by AI-powered technology while considering young adults' needs, concerns, and goals. The study's recommended communication model was Berlo's SMCR communication model, which aimed to foster positive connections between young adults and AI technology while promoting well-being and personal development. Berlo's SMCR communication model is a well-established communication paradigm that can be adapted to address the issues associated with AI-powered technology and young adults (Farjana et al., 2023). Let us explore how Berlo's SMCR communication model can be modified to align more closely with this context.

Source

In the context of AI and young adults, the term 'source' encompasses the individuals who create and curate online content and the AI algorithms responsible for generating and recommending information. The adaptation emphasizes the importance of generating and curating ethical content (P. Lee et al., 2022). Encouraging AI programmers to prioritize transparency and avoid biases when developing algorithmic content suggestions is crucial.

Message

Whether delivered by humans or AI, the content's 'message' includes any potential impact it may have on the perceptions and behaviors of young adults. The adaptation in this aspect promotes the dissemination of accurate, enlightening, and informative content. Encouraging platforms employing AI to make content selection and customization transparent is vital, enabling users to make informed decisions.

Channel

The term 'channel' refers to the medium used for communication, including social networking sites, messaging services, and other online platforms. The adaptation here is to encourage young adults to make thoughtful channel choices while considering their well-being. Advising them on managing notifications and establishing appropriate technological limits can contribute to healthier AI interactions.

Receiver

The audience receiving the communication—in this case, young adults engaging with AI-generated content—is called the 'receiver.' The adaptation in this context involves equipping young adults with the analytical tools they need to evaluate information generated by AI (Rutledge, 2021). It empowers them to investigate the sources of information and engage in deliberate discussions regarding the impact of AI. While Berlo's original SMCR communication model may not explicitly address it, incorporating feedback is crucial when discussing AI and young adults (Muyanga & Phiri, 2021).

The adaptation includes establishing a feedback loop where teenagers can share their opinions and experiences with AI. Encouraging platforms to leverage user input to enhance content suggestions and AI algorithms is essential. The broader context of AI's impact on the lives of young adults, including areas such as employment, mental health, privacy, and career development, must be considered within the revised model (Bubica & Boljat, 2022). The adaptation includes incorporating 'context' as a crucial component. It entails discussing the broader implications of AI on communication, encompassing issues like job displacement, algorithmic biases, and ethical concerns.

Ethical Considerations

Ethical considerations regarding AI, mainly responsible AI usage, data privacy, and accountability, should be emphasized in the updated model. The adaptation involves encouraging both AI developers and young adults to make ethical decisions by integrating ethical considerations as a cross-cutting factor throughout the model (Parijkova, 2021). In summary, the study sought to provide young adults with a framework for navigating AI-powered communication successfully. It is achieved by adapting Berlo's SMCR communication model, which focuses on ethical content creation, transparency, critical thinking, and feedback integration. These modifications ensure that young adults engage with AI in a manner that supports their well-being, personal development, and ethical principles.

Revamping Communication: The Need for a Remodel

While young adults may demonstrate more digital skills, the workplace and society must regulate technology usage to maintain a healthy balance and encourage responsible digital citizenship (Van Berkel et al., 2023). Today, where digital abilities are highly prized, technology has become indispensable for everyone (Akyol, 2023). Despite the numerous advantages of technology, society must oversee how young adults utilize it. To further support this claim, the study considered the following factors.

Responsible Digital Citizens

The first factor to consider is the digital age's tremendous learning, creativity, and communication prospects. Young adults should be responsible digital citizens who understand the importance of ethical behavior, online safety, and courteous online interactions, which require regulating and monitoring their technology use. The second factor is balancing screen time with other activities, especially given the abundance of digital devices and platforms available. Excessive screen time can lead to social isolation, sleep problems, and sedentary lifestyles (Deng & Li, 2022).

By setting boundaries and promoting a healthy balance between online and offline activities, we can encourage physical exercise, in-person interactions, and well-rounded growth in young learners (e.g., the blue light effects on the eyes). Screens, including those on computers, tablets, and smartphones, produce blue light, which can interfere with sleep cycles and tire young adults (H. Lee et al., 2017).

Blue Light Effect

It is primarily because of its effect on the melatonin hormone (N. A. Wong & Bahmani, 2022). The pineal gland in the brain secretes the hormone melatonin, which is essential for controlling the sleep-wake cycle. Exposure to light, incredibly blue and natural light, affects the generation of melatonin (N. A. Wong & Bahmani, 2022). Natural sunshine contains much blue light, which tells the brain it is daytime. Young adults are kept awake and vigilant during the day by this blue light exposure, which suppresses melatonin synthesis (N. A. Wong & Bahmani, 2022).

The problem occurs when young adults are exposed to artificial blue light sources, particularly at night and in the evening. Because screens release light, extended nighttime screen use can disrupt the body's ability to produce melatonin. This process makes it harder for young adults to sleep at night. The normal cycle of sleep and wakefulness might be disturbed, making it difficult to fall and stay asleep, leading to poor quality sleep and affecting their health and career (H. Lee et al., 2017).

Increased daytime tiredness and weariness might affect work efficiency and quality. It is the same for young adults' health. Sleep deprivation impairs the body's capacity to repair and rejuvenate, resulting in fatigue and decreased attentiveness. To lessen the adverse effects of blue light from screens on sleep cycles, young adults can think about limiting their time spent on screens, especially the hour or two before bed. Young adults may encourage improved sleep hygiene and support their regular sleep-wake cycles by carefully monitoring their screen time, particularly in the evening (N. A. Wong & Bahmani, 2022). Another need is to bring out the SMCR communication remodel.

Health and Well-Being

Young adults' mental health and well-being can be significantly impacted by their constant connectedness and exposure to social media (Niknejad et al., 2020). Excessive AI-powered technology use can increase anxiety, low self-esteem, and cyberbullying (Park, 2020). Young adults should be encouraged to develop critical thinking skills. Professionals and colleagues can promote media literacy, engage in discussions about trustworthy and false information, and equip young adults with the skills to use the internet responsibly, one objective of bringing up SMCR communication remodel (Heller, 2012).

It is crucial that real-world experiences complement technology rather than replace it (Friederich et al., 2024). Offline activities that young adults engage in should include physical play, outdoor exploration, reading, hobbies, and quality time spent with co-workers, family, colleagues, and friends. Striking this balance benefits youth by fostering critical social skills, creativity, imagination, and a well-rounded worldview (Rai et al., 2017).

Despite young adults' advanced digital skills, they must exercise control and oversight over technology use. In doing so, young adults and society can promote responsible online behavior, balance screen time and other pursuits, safeguard mental health, encourage critical thinking, and ensure the holistic development of young adults in our digital society (Deng & Li, 2022). The SMCR Communication may highlight the need to develop face-to-face rather than online communication.

Self-Guidance

While multimedia offers entertainment, education, and self-expression opportunities, young adults should exercise control and monitor their access to information (Korol & Bevelander, 2021). Self-guidance and self-control are essential prerequisites before embracing the SMCR communication remodel. The importance of balancing digital and in-person relationships cannot be overstated, even in the era of text-based communication. Face-to-face interactions offer opportunities to develop social skills, practice active listening, and nurture empathy—essential elements for forging deep connections, understanding different perspectives, and building trusting interpersonal relationships. Notably, young adults tend to consume videos as their primary source of entertainment more than at work or during their education (Rao & Lingam, 2021). They watch videos on learning websites, streaming services, and platforms like YouTube and Instagram reels. Simultaneously, these young adults are growing up in a society that highly values gaming (Danet, 2020).

The New Culture

They can access various age-appropriate video games on multiple devices, including consoles, laptops, and mobile devices. Whether for better or worse, the act of gaming on devices is controversial, and the study examined the experiences of young adults. AI systems analyze individuals' online activities, preferences, and behaviors. Young adults engage with information that aligns with their interests, increasing the likelihood of frequent use of social media platforms (Hong et al., 2021). AI-powered recommendation engines present users with friends, groups, pages, and information they might find interesting.

It can strengthen young adults' social relationships and introduce them to fresh cultures and viewpoints. AI technologies also track user interaction metrics such as likes, shares, comments, and views (Kaspi & Venkatraman, 2023). Through these indicators, young adults may seek validation and boost their self-esteem, leading to behavior patterns that prioritize engaging with their posts. AI-powered chatbots offer instant customer support, which can be advantageous for young adults seeking rapid and effective interactions while seeking assistance or information from companies or service providers.

Social Media Influencers

AI can also identify influencers whose content aligns with the interests of young adults (H. Lee et al., 2017). Influencer marketing has gained popularity, with reputable social media influencers promoting goods and services. Concerns have been raised about the effects of young adults' constant use of social media, exacerbated by AI's ability to capture attention. Algorithms designed to keep young adults engaged could exacerbate issues related to anxiety, addiction, and feelings of inadequacy (Terzopoulos & Satratzemi, 2020).

The intersection of AI-powered technology and social media has transformed how young adults communicate, consume content, and express themselves online. It offers tailored opportunities and experiences but raises concerns about bias, mental health, and privacy. It is crucial to balance the benefits of AI-driven advancements with ethical considerations and user well-being, and it is essential to understand the need for a communication remodel.

Social Networking

In professional contexts, social networking, workplace behavior, and AI technology strongly influence young adults' actions, attitudes, and experiences. Young adults can access social networking sites, facilitating interaction with classmates, mentors, and professionals (Karusala, 2022). AI-enabled algorithms simplify the process of finding relevant connections and content. Platforms like LinkedIn enable young adults to expand their professional networks, access industry knowledge, and stay informed about trends. AI algorithms partially determine the content a user's network sees (Terzopoulos & Satratzemi, 2020).

Therefore, young adults must carefully curate their online profiles to align with their brand. Through thoughtful content creation and engagement on social media, they can establish authority and competence in their respective fields. Young adults are increasingly using social media for job hunting and recruitment. AI-powered systems can evaluate job applications and profiles to match candidates with suitable positions, streamlining the hiring process for employers and job seekers. It identified the need to implement a communication remodel due to these identified issues that can directly harm the business.

Remote Work Experience

AI technology has also enhanced collaboration and remote work for young adults. They utilize AI-driven communication tools, project management software, and virtual assistants when collaborating with colleagues across different regions and time zones. Educational materials and online learning systems powered by AI are frequently shared on social media platforms, enabling young adults to access resources and courses that help them stay competitive in the job market (Terzopoulos & Satratzemi, 2020).

However, the lines between work and personal life may blur due to the widespread use of social networking and AI-powered tools, necessitating the establishment of clear boundaries and responsible technology usage habits. Employers may utilize AI technology for various tasks, including monitoring employee behavior and productivity, which may raise privacy concerns and stress among young adults who feel continuously monitored. Young adults must follow the rules of digital etiquette while using social media for work (C. Y. Chen et al., 2022). Building a solid professional reputation requires individuals to be mindful.

Analyzing the Business Implications of Communication Remodeling

There are various advantages to extending and customizing the SMCR (Source, Message, Channel, Receiver) model to accommodate Young adults' unique demands and difficulties in their personal and professional lives (Koubaa et al., 2023). It can assist young adults with company management in the following ways (Balakrishnan et al., 2021). They are achieving better communication in young adults.

Digital Literacy

By modifying the SMCR communication model to consider digital literacy, young adults will be more equipped to manage the digital world. Encourage young adults to think critically about the messages they see online so they may make educated decisions and steer clear of false information (Koubaa et al., 2023). Young adults are better equipped to comprehend the different accessible online communication channels, including social media, websites, and messaging platforms, by considering digital literacy within the SMCR model. Its comprehension allows them to recognize dependable information sources and differentiate between accurate and false information (Koubaa et al., 2023). Through the SMCR model's promotion of digital literacy, young adults are more conscious of online communication's possible dangers, including identity theft, cyberbullying, and privacy violations.

Young adults become less susceptible to online attacks as they learn to protect their private data, online reputation, and privacy settings. Young individuals with digital literacy abilities feel equipped to interact with internet information responsibly and discernibly (Koubaa et al., 2023). They know the significance of fact-checking sources, confirming facts, and considering opposing viewpoints before formulating opinions or disseminating content. By including digital literacy in the SMCR communication paradigm, young adults are better equipped to navigate the digital world. By promoting critical thinking, responsible participation, and safeguarding against online threats, this adjustment gives young individuals the knowledge and abilities needed to move confidently and honorably within the digital environment.

Emotional Intelligence

Emotional intelligence is a component of human development that can assist young adults in understanding and controlling their emotions in social and professional contexts (Heller, 2012). By comprehending and managing their emotions, young adults may efficiently handle stress, impulses, and reactions in various settings. Their capacity for self-control improves their capacity for making decisions and builds resilience in the face of difficulties, both in social and professional contexts. Effective leadership requires a high degree of emotional intelligence. Emotionally intelligent young adults are better able to lead by example, inspire and encourage others, and form cohesive teams (Heller, 2012).

Young adults can influence stakeholders, maneuver through organizational politics, and promote constructive change in their professional lives (Lachmann et al., 2019). Young adults between 18 and 25 who possess emotional intelligence are more equipped to comprehend and manage their emotions, deal with social and professional obstacles, form lasting relationships, and succeed personally and professionally. Emotional intelligence is a crucial aspect of human growth. By developing their emotional intelligence abilities, young adults may realize their full potential and prosper in today's fast-paced, globally interconnected world.

Resolution of Conflict

Resolution of conflict using good negotiating and conflict resolution techniques may improve interpersonal relationships and workplace dynamics. Including networking and relationship-building abilities in the model can help young adults advance in their jobs (Lai et al., 2021). Integrating the fundamentals of leadership communication can help prepare young adults for leadership positions. The capacity to acquire and use new communication technologies and tools and the model's emphasis on adaptation can benefit young adults when they join the profession (Heller, 2012).

Managers and business leaders may learn how to promote successful communication within teams and across organizational hierarchies using a modified SMCR model. Organizations may negotiate transitions and transformations more efficiently by considering communication in the context of change management (Karusala, 2022). Information management and data-driven decision-making components can be integrated to help managers make well-informed decisions.

Customer Relationship

Customer interactions may be enhanced by extending the model to incorporate customer feedback loops and communication channels. A modernized model can assist companies and professionals in keeping up with new communication trends and technology (Behizadeh et al., 2023). Including negotiation and conflict resolution techniques in the model can aid in resolving conflicts and promoting cooperation. Preparing young adults and company managers for effective crisis communication is crucial in today's fast-paced, interconnected world (Lachmann et al., 2019). Including leadership communication abilities in the model's expansion will help managers and other leaders better manage their teams. The SMCR communication remodel can assist firms in navigating change more quickly.

Effective communication is essential during times of change (Karusala, 2022). Streamlined processes, productivity, and effectiveness businesses may locate and eliminate communication bottlenecks and inefficiencies using the SMCR paradigm. Businesses may allocate duties and responsibilities more efficiently by understanding how information is transmitted and received. Adapting the concept might help develop and uphold a consistent brand message across numerous communication channels for brand and image management (Elhajjar et al., 2023).

Comprehensive knowledge of communication dynamics is necessary for developing an effective public relations strategy. The approach may be developed to meet the difficulties and complexities of cross-cultural communication, which is crucial in the current global corporate world. The approach can aid organizations in controlling the flow of information and utilizing data to make wise decisions.

Communication Ethics

The ethics in communication approach can help firms retain honesty and openness in their communication methods by considering ethical factors (Karusala, 2022). The SMCR communication model may be modified and expanded to address the issues and possibilities of AI-powered technology and the digital era. It can be helpful for both company management and young adults. The strategy can promote efficiency and success on the personal and professional levels by improving young adults' communication skills and assisting organizations in streamlining their communication procedures. Effective communication is essential for success in today's quickly changing world (Lachmann et al., 2019). A revamped communication approach may help young adults and organizations thrive in this setting.

Summary

The study explored the complex connection that young adults have with AI-powered technology, essentially highlighting the need for a new communication paradigm to accommodate the changing nature of communication due to technological breakthroughs, particularly AI. These improvements may be implemented and utilized from a practical business perspective in organizational situations. In summary, the study explored the implications of AI-powered technology on young adults, stressing the benefits it offers to this group of young adults while also looking at potential drawbacks.

The study traced the beginnings of Berlo's SMCR communication model and outlines its components, highlighting the need for a revised communication model. The research highlights the shortcomings of the current paradigm and makes the case for a thorough redesign of communication that considers AI's revolutionary impact. Its planned makeover is significant from a business perspective since it provides insights into how firms might use these changes for improved communication, more efficiency, and a competitive edge in the rapidly changing technology world. The study advances our knowledge of the complex relationships between young adults, AI-powered technology, and the communication systems that support them.

CHAPTER THREE: METHODOLOGY

The qualitative study investigated the viewpoints, experiences, and goals of young people in Torrance, California, between the ages of 18 and 25. The study investigated this demographic group's social, economic, cultural, and personal narratives to shed light on its many facets by using the Zoom audio-only interview instrument. The research documented the depth and diversity of perspectives within this dynamic age group using an open-ended approach. Policymakers, educators, and community leaders may be able to tailor interventions and support systems better to meet the changing needs of young people in Torrance in LA County with the help of the insights obtained from this study. The stage of life between 18 and 25 is characterized by decision-making, identity-building, and exploration for young adults.

Profound changes in the individual and the larger society characterize the crucial time between late adolescence and adulthood. LA County, well-known for its thriving arts and business prospects, provides a distinctive context for comprehending the experiences of this particular demographic (Hekkala & Hekkala, 2021). Despite its diversity and vibrancy, the views and viewpoints of young adults in this region helped collect quality data. By doing qualitative research into the goals and actual experiences of young adults toward their usage of AI powered devices in Torrance, this research aims to close the gap that is identified in the problem statement, the potential business ramifications of excessive screen time and digital overload of young adults aged 18 to 25.

Methodology

The study investigated and validated its findings methodically to identify the implications of AI-powered technology on young adults aged 18 to 25 and to recognize the need for a communication remodel to overcome business ramifications. The research design organized the study, providing a detailed analysis of the benefits and drawbacks of AI integration for young adults. The target population of 18 to 25-year-old young adults was adequately defined using a planned data-gathering procedure.

The research collected a variety of viewpoints about the implications of AI. A thorough data analysis, including qualitative elements, was carried out to draw insightful conclusions (Pavlíková et al., 2023). Upholding the validity and credibility of the study required acknowledging presumptions and guaranteeing the reliability of the research findings to meet the ultimate objective of the study, which was to build a successful communication method that positively affects business.

The methodological approach offers a solid basis for comprehending the intricate interactions between AI, communication models, and young adults' experiences. The target group aged 18 to 25, categorized as 'young adults,' develops in an increasingly digital world. It is imperative to identify and address potential challenges and behavioral consequences technology may have on them (Holland et al., 2021). By identifying and researching the challenges associated with the prolonged use of technology, the research may design effective strategies to promote healthy behavioral development and reduce any possible negative impacts that can bring positive outcomes to businesses through young adults' positive communication reactions.

Therefore, the problem statement calls for creating tactics that encourage responsible and balanced AI-powered technology usage and assist in developing desirable behavioral outcomes. As identified in the problem statement, it was essential to research the future implications of AI-powered technology on young adults as it impacts business. Interviews were used in a qualitative research design to collect primary data for this study. The target group was young adults (18 to 25 years old) who lived in Torrance, LA County, California.

Challenges and Difficulties

The study determined the obstacles and possible outcomes in social interaction, cognitive development, emotional stability, physical health, and digital citizenship and how this impacts business. Excessive screen time and digital overload refer to the overuse of AI-powered device screens, including those on computers, tablets, smartphones, smartwatches, and other digital devices (Mollborn et al., 2021). The problem occurs when young individuals spend a significant portion of the day interacting with screens for work, communication, entertainment, or education—often at the expense of other essential activities and aspects of their lives (Okeke et al., 2018).

Moreover, a sedentary lifestyle brought on by young adults' excessive screen time might increase the risk of obesity, cardiovascular disease, and musculoskeletal disorders, as well as limit possibilities for exercise, which again impacts personal well-being and then the workplace where it affects business negatively (Terzopoulos & Satratzemi, 2020). When young adults are not physically well enough to concentrate on work, the whole situation changes and brings about efficiency and effectiveness of work.

Digital screen time entails much sitting and little exercise, which may be detrimental to the physical health of young adults. Once this impacts young adults' health, they will not be able to attend work, their attention span for their job will be less, and their productivity level will go down, again affecting business. The entire procedure might take some time, but it is evident that the root cause of this effect is AI-powered device usage, which will reduce the effectiveness of the business. The difficulties young individuals have developing cognitively due to using smart devices is another important aspect. Excessive screen usage may hinder cognitive development by reducing opportunities for creative play, experiential learning, and problem-solving, which are crucial for developing critical thinking, creativity, and problem-solving skills (Terzopoulos & Satratzemi, 2020). Young adults may find it more challenging to focus and pay attention when using digital devices since they are accustomed to the constant stimulation and instant gratification they provide. Nevertheless, introducing a communication remodel mitigates these limitations (Mollborn et al., 2021).

It might make concentrating and focusing harder when doing tasks requiring sustained concentration, including jobs or offline hobbies. It might be challenging to fall asleep and obtain enough restorative sleep while using screens before bed or at night (Prasad & Quinones, 2020). Because blue light from screens interferes with melatonin, a hormone that regulates sleep cycles, it may cause sleep disorders and increase tiredness (Pullen Sansfaçon et al., 2022). Excessive screen time might impair a person's social interaction and communication capacity, primarily affecting business in the long term.

These young adults may spend less time completing job responsibilities on time, quality and practical work, forming relationships, engaging in face-to-face interactions, and picking up social skills like empathy, active listening, and nonverbal communication, which again narrow down their ability to work well in their career and that affects business more broadly. The researcher discussed not only one young adult but the entire age group, and the ramifications to business was huge when considering the target population.

Research Design

The research was motivated by an investigation of the complex network of difficulties, effects, and ramifications that AI-powered technology poses for the conduct of young adults between the ages of 18 and 25. It aimed to understand better how AI-powered technology affects and changes many elements of young adults' behavior, focusing on examining the possible consequences. These characteristics include workplace ethics, social interaction, mental growth, emotional stability, physical well-being, and digital citizenship (Pavlíková et al., 2023).

By carefully examining the aspects, it intends to shed light on technology's positive and negative transformational effects on young adults' lives. It acknowledges the urgent need to understand how this revolutionary force shapes the behaviors of the young adult generation in an era dominated by digital interactions and the pervasiveness of AI-powered technologies (Rubino et al., 2022).

The research study hoped to demonstrate the need for an updated model that more accurately captures the nuances of communication in the digital era by analyzing the history and tenets of Berlo's SMCR communication model. Beyond theory, this research examined real-world applications by reviewing how the updated communication model, also known as the Communication Remodel, can be used from a business perspective, particularly when interacting with young adults.

Additionally, the study aimed to clarify the significant influence of AI-powered technology on young adults' growth and well-being, as well as on business and its long run. It acknowledged the necessity for a communication model to appropriately explain how interaction patterns change in the digital sphere. The research aimed to offer academically stimulating and practically relevant insights, adding to a deeper understanding of the complex relationship between young adults, technology, and communication models.

It does this by utilizing rigorous methodology and diverse sources. Businesses may better engage and connect with this group by integrating the findings from the study with the SMCR model adaption (Sakib et al., 2023). It helped them prepare for the communication landscape that will change young adults' attitudes, attributes, and work ethics, allowing them to balance their needs in life and work and reducing business circumstances.

Qualitative Research Method

The main reason for selecting qualitative methodology in the research was its exploratory nature. The topic the researcher discussed was timely and a current trend. Therefore, exploration takes place throughout the study. Another reason to choose qualitative research was that it was frequently used to investigate novel or developing subjects or develop a deeper comprehension of a phenomenon (Mohamud et al., 2023).

When the subject was unknown, it was beneficial and non-numerical, where the researcher did not focus on quantity or numbers but on the actual situations, incidents, personal experiences, and ideas of one's life when it relates to AI-powered devices and their usage. According to the qualitative method, understanding the environment in which the study is conducted is essential (Korol & Bevelander, 2021). It entails considering cultural, social, historical, and environmental aspects that might impact the phenomena under study.

Reason to Use Qualitative Research

Moreover, qualitative research highlights the advantages of AI-powered communication devices by finding examples of how technology has facilitated relationships, increased communication effectiveness, or improved social interactions (Cammers-Goodwin, 2023). By considering diverse contexts such as the workplace, classroom, or social gatherings, qualitative studies help academics better comprehend the contexts that affect how AI-powered communication devices are used (Volgger et al., 2022). Using qualitative research, a new communication strategy catering to young adults' wants and needs is developed. The study gathered user feedback on possible model revisions through interviews or usability testing, ensuring that the model aligned with users' preferences and expectations.

Best practices for employing AI-powered devices for communication were determined using qualitative data teaching techniques young adults find useful for preserving meaningful connections and enhancing communication while employing technology. Qualitative findings can guide revamping the existing communication strategy tailored to young adults' specific wants and needs (C. Kang et al., 2023). The study obtained user feedback on potential model revisions through online interviews. Young adults better understand AI-driven apps' usefulness, accuracy, and appropriateness in social interactions (Hasasneh et al., 2023). Employing AI-powered devices for communication is enriched by determining best practices through qualitative data.

The study imparted techniques that young adults found useful for preserving meaningful connections and enhancing communication while utilizing technology. However, qualitative research may uncover challenges in implementing a new communication model. The study delved into the influence of young adult well-being on communication practices and technology adoption using qualitative approaches, examining how their behavior shapes their decisions regarding the well-being of the work environment. A qualitative longitudinal study demonstrates how young adults' communication styles evolve as they adapt to new communication paradigms and AI-powered devices where they can mitigate the adverse effects that cause the business (Balcombe & De Leo, 2022).

The researcher moved on to understanding how a revised communication model mitigates the effects of AI-powered devices while maximizing the benefits for young adults' social interactions and communication skills to improve their work. Qualitative research methodologies significantly aid in understanding how a new communication model might minimize the negative impacts of AI-powered smart devices while emphasizing the advantages for young adults' social connections and communication abilities (Lynch et al., 2023). Finally, the approach enabled the study to acquire comprehensive information, understand user viewpoints, and gain contextual knowledge essential for designing a new communication model that maximizes advantages and minimizes potential drawbacks to business.

Creating Theories

Qualitative research may offer a wealth of information to enable the creation of such hypotheses when a researcher wishes to create a model or theory to explain a phenomenon. Qualitative research can assist in assessing the efficacy of programs or treatments and creating theories by gathering input from participants, stakeholders, or experts. Qualitative research may offer a wealth of information to enable the creation of such hypotheses when a researcher wishes to create a model or theory to explain phenomena (B. Lee et al., 2022).

Intervention Evaluation

Qualitative research can assist in assessing the efficacy of programs or treatments by gathering input from participants, stakeholders, or experts. Qualitative research is best suited when a study issue is exploratory, complicated, subjective, theoretical, or evaluative. Interviews encourage participants to express their ideas and experiences on their terms, frequently resulting in more thorough answers without taking much time. With interviews, participants are more accessible to answer in a way that makes sense through their experiences, frequently revealing essential details that the researcher would have missed (Bruckermann et al., 2022).

To get insights into complicated situations, the researcher must better grasp the participant's viewpoints, beliefs, attitudes, and experiences, which is why interviews are essential. Interviews can elicit surprising answers and provide fresh data. Participants may raise subjects or viewpoints that the researcher had not considered when they are allowed to express themselves in their own words freely (Bruckermann et al., 2022). By asking open-ended questions through online audio-only Zoom interviews, the researcher may establish a connection with the subject, express interest in their answers, and provide them with a safe space to talk about their experiences without fear of being judged.

Insights and Perceptions

As a result, participants may have a favorable study experience, raising the possibility of continuing to participate in future studies. By allowing individuals to share their unique viewpoints and experiences, researchers may assess how closely or differently these replies match current ideas. If the participant data are consistent with the theories, this can supplement the evidence. However, if the evidence deviates from accepted beliefs, this may point to the need for more research or a modification of the available knowledge.

As J. Kim (2020) outlined, self-reporting interview questionnaires represent a systematic approach to collecting data, typically encompassing a series of inquiries designed to extract participants' data, viewpoints, or attitudes. The process of data collection through interviews involves several key steps. Firstly, in the design phase, the research formulated a series of inquiries relevant to the subject matter under investigation. Respondents can answer interview questions and offer detailed explanations. Next, recruiting participants involves selecting a sample from the intended audience. The study focused on young adults in Torrance, LA County, California, specifically those between 18 and 25 years old as the sample.

The subsequent step involved online Zoom interviews with participants. Participants respond to the questions right away, answering according to their preferences. As identified, qualitative research plays a significant role in understanding and assessing the integration of AI-powered technology into young adults' well-being and interpersonal relationships, and through a direct interview method. It is effective that the researcher can gather timely and realistic information about the ideas and thoughts of these young adults towards their usage of AI-powered devices at workplace (Bruckermann et al., 2022).

It enables a thorough investigation of young adults' encounters with AI technology, capturing the depth of their experiences and how technology affects their relationships and well-being through interviews. Qualitative methodologies explore the contextual aspects of how AI technology affects young adults, considering cultural, social, economic, and personal factors influencing their engagement with these technologies and how those interactions affect their relationships and general well-being (P. Lee et al., 2022). Identifying the intricate processes that AI technology employs to influence young adults' relationships and general well-being is facilitated by qualitative research, providing a detailed perspective on mediating and moderating elements.

Furthermore, qualitative studies excel in uncovering the unforeseen effects of integrating AI technology (Bruckermann et al., 2022). The study learns how specific aspects or applications of technology, unintended in the first place, affect the relationships and lifestyles of young adults. The interview approach provides insight into coping mechanisms young adults employ to deal with potential difficulties using AI-powered technologies, thereby improving interventions and support systems (Bruckermann et al., 2022). Diverse viewpoints are captured through qualitative research, allowing an examination of perspectives among young adults based on variables like age, gender, financial level, and cultural background.

Impacts and Effectiveness

Findings from qualitative research may be used to generate design concepts, rules, and recommendations for AI-powered technologies, pointing out areas where ethical considerations, privacy issues, or user experiences must be addressed to promote young adults' well-being and good relationships. The longitudinal perspective of qualitative research offers insightful information on trends and developmental processes as young adults' usage of AI technology evolves. The human-centered approach prioritizes young adults' voices and experiences, ensuring that their viewpoints shape the conversation on how technology affects their relationships and well-being (Bruckermann et al., 2022).

Conclusively, qualitative research is essential for acquiring a more profound and complex understanding of how incorporating AI-powered technologies impacts business through young adults' well-being. It offers the qualitative information required to supplement quantitative research, informs approaches for fostering successful outcomes, and addresses potential difficulties. In this context, conducting qualitative research using an interview helps understand young adults' communication practices and issues with AI-powered devices (Bruckermann et al., 2022).

The study pinpointed problems and areas that required a change, and through qualitative research and its results, the researcher identified the negative consequences of excessive AI-powered technology usage and how it impacts one's life and the business directly. All the components of a good work environment are based on young adults' social relationships, communication abilities, and work ethics, which will finally bridge the gap of the study to bring a communication remodel for the well-being of business (C. Y. Chen et al., 2022).

Research Instruments

The research contained an open-source preexisting questionnaire instrument to meet the success criteria of qualitative research. The study sought to add new perspectives to the body of knowledge on youth development and well-being by elevating the voices and experiences of Torrance young adults ages 18 to 25. The study aimed to get comprehensive support and empowerment of young people in Torrance, California city, by providing evidence through the results of an interview conducted to gather young adults' viewpoints, struggles, and goals regarding their usage of AI-powered devices and their ideas on how much harm this will bring to their workplace. The plan was to obtain online audio-only Zoom interviews with the 15 participants, the target audience, ages 18 to 25, by asking open-ended questions to gather information about young adults' interactions and usage of smart devices.

Using the identified target population means believing their contributions and viewpoints was helpful and supportive evidence for the research (Chali et al., 2022). The researcher analyzed data using Python for coding, themes, patterns, visualization, and interpretations. Small sample sizes are standard in qualitative investigations, but obtaining statistical representativeness is not the primary goal. Instead, the study tried to pick subjects or situations that may offer deep and varied perspectives on the research issue. It is beneficial when the study tries to find 'how' and 'why' answers and when the researcher wants to record the viewpoints and real-life experiences of the target group (Chennouk et al., 2022).

Through online Zoom interviews, the study helped understand the actual experiences of the target audience and their opinions. Research needs to ensure that every participant is exposed to the same stimuli by carefully crafting the questions, which will increase the consistency of the results (Mohamud et al., 2023). By allowing participants to voice their ideas and opinions, the interview offers a complete understanding of the target audience's expectations, worries, and points of view on AI-powered device usage, workplace responsibilities, and the need for a communication model.

The research's findings can help develop strategies, policies, and communication tactics that address young adults' unique requirements and preferences in the context of AI to introduce a communication model and mitigate the business implications. Exploring subjective feelings and perceptions is a good use of this methodology. Young adults' potential reach and diversity on social media platforms like Facebook, WhatsApp, TikTok, Messenger, Twitter, LinkedIn, Snapchat, and Instagram can lead to a broader range of replies (Borna et al., 2023). It might improve how broadly applicable the results are.

Honesty is encouraged by anonymity (Bruckermann et al., 2022). Responding to online Zoom interviews is expected to be more honest and open about the interviewer's experiences and opinions since they may feel more at ease disclosing sensitive material without worrying about criticism. Unlike other data collection methods, online Zoom interviews might be more efficient, effective, and affordable. The qualitative study aligned with the planned and research objectives and the research findings could support the creation of a communication model, which is the ultimate goal of minimizing communication barriers to business.

Target Population

The 18 to 25 age range was chosen for the study of AI-powered technology usage and the necessity for a communication remodel based on several factors, including young adults' communication preferences, technological adaption, and developmental stage. These were a few of the reasons. Young adults between 18 and 25 are called digital natives since they were raised in a technologically advanced world. They are more likely to be accustomed to and at ease with

AI-powered devices in their regular routines. These people are at a time when they are moving from late adolescence to adulthood. They frequently make important decisions affecting their future (J. Kim, 2020).

Accessibility and Flexibility: Young adults may participate in education and skill development at their own pace and convenience, thanks to the unparalleled accessibility and flexibility of AI-powered online and technology-based learning platforms. AI-powered instructional technologies provide chances for ongoing learning and professional development, regardless of how people juggle jobs, school, or other responsibilities (Engwerda et al., 2023).

Customized Learning Experiences: AI systems examine learner information, preferences, and performance indicators to provide young adults with individualized learning experiences suited to their unique requirements and preferences. AI is used by virtual mentors, intelligent tutoring systems, and adaptive learning platforms to improve the efficacy and efficiency of education delivery by offering targeted interventions, enrichment, and remediation opportunities (Engwerda et al., 2023).

Enhanced Learner Engagement and Retention: Interactive simulations, gamification components, and multimedia material are all included in AI-powered educational solutions. NLP, sentiment analysis, and affective computing are just a few methods that AI-driven platforms might use to gauge learners' emotional states, modify material delivery, and provide a safe and engaging learning environment (Engwerda et al., 2023).

Skill Development for the Future Workforce: In a technology-driven economy, developing AI-related abilities is becoming increasingly critical for young adults as they prepare to enter the workforce or progress in their professions. With AI-powered learning resources, young adults may become proficient in programming, ML, data analysis, and digital literacy, giving them the skills they need to flourish in various professional settings (Engwerda et al., 2023).

Alignment with Workplace Trends: AI technology in education is consistent with the increasing ubiquity of these technologies in business and the workplace. Institutions may better prepare young adults for the demands of the modern workforce, where AI-driven automation, data analytics, and decision support systems are increasingly pervasive, by exposing them to AI-powered tools and techniques early in their educational path.

Creativity and Entrepreneurship: AI-driven educational tools support creativity and entrepreneurship and prepare young individuals for conventional career paths. AI-driven education promotes innovative ideas and entrepreneurial attitudes by enabling students to solve problems creatively, use new technology, and investigate multidisciplinary fields (Korchi, 2023).

Researching AI-powered educational technology is essential for young individuals between 18 and 25 since it may help them with their academic pursuits, career transitions, or start-up endeavors. Educational institutions and students alike can harness the transformative potential of AI to drive personalized learning experiences, enhance workforce readiness, foster innovation, and adapt to the changing demands of the digital age by embracing online and technology-based learning modalities infused with AI capabilities (Bruckermann et al., 2022).

Professional Group

Young adults are either about to enter the workforce or are completing higher education. Understanding how AI technologies are used is essential for professional growth and flexibility in the modern workplace since these technologies are incorporated into various professions. Generally, people in this age range are more able to adjust to new technology. They can pick up the usage of and rapidly incorporate AI-powered products into their personal and professional life, making them likely to be early adopters (Korchi, 2023).

AI technologies are used in various professions and sectors, including marketing, finance, healthcare, and education. The need for people with expertise in AI-related fields, including ML, data analysis, NLP, and algorithm creation, is rising as AI technologies proliferate in the workplace (Korchi, 2023). By obtaining these skills through specialized courses, certificates, and practical training programs, young adults can improve their employability and employment prospects.

Automation solutions driven by AI reduce duplication, enhance processes, and boost productivity in various sectors (Chennouk et al., 2022). Knowing how AI can automate repetitive jobs may free up time and resources for young individuals just entering the workforce, enabling them to concentrate on more intricate and strategic parts of their roles. AI-powered career portals use their users' abilities, interests, and desired careers to connect young adults with internships, jobs, and mentoring programs. To broaden their professional networks and consider other career routes, young professionals may engage with peers, industry experts, and future employers using these platforms (Chennouk et al., 2022).

Understanding how AI technologies are applied in different professions may be pretty beneficial for young adults who are either developing in their jobs or getting ready to enter the workforce. Young professionals can position themselves for success and contribute to the evolution of the AI-driven workplace by learning AI-related skills, utilizing automation tools, making data-driven decisions, utilizing personalized learning opportunities, networking efficiently, and thinking about the ethical implications of their actions (Chennouk et al., 2022).

Communication Preferences

Young adults frequently prefer digital and tech-savvy communication platforms. AI-powered communication tools and platforms cater to these tastes; therefore, it makes sense to investigate communication remodeling in this age range (Chennouk et al., 2022). Young people are frequently defined by their comfort and familiarity with digital technology, especially those between 18 and 25. They are used to integrating digital tools and platforms into many parts of their lives, including communication, having grown up at a time when technology is pervasive. As a result, individuals frequently choose communication channels based on connectedness, efficiency, and ease of use.

Young adults are drawn to the features and capabilities of AI-powered communication products and platforms (Kosiyaporn et al., 2022). These AI-powered technologies improve user experiences, expedite communication, and customize interactions. Examining communication remodeling in this age group is essential since young adults have embraced digital and tech-savvy communication channels widely.

Gaining knowledge on how AI-driven communication tools affect communication preferences, patterns, and behaviors might help understand how the dynamics of interpersonal interactions are changing in the digital age (Kosiyaporn et al., 2022). Furthermore, investigating how relationships, social norms, and the spread of information may be impacted by AI-driven communication might help redesign and rebuild the existing communication system that is more suited to the requirements and preferences of young people in the future.

Influence on Future Trends

The generation that will drive technological developments and societal transformations is represented by young adults. Understanding how AI technologies impact their communication habits might help predict future trends and preferences. AI-powered communication tools are among the many new technologies that young adults frequently adopt first. Researchers and industry stakeholders can obtain valuable insights into the AI technologies that will likely be widely adopted by analyzing their usage patterns and behaviors. Early adulthood shapes communication patterns that frequently carry over into subsequent life phases. Therefore, knowing how AI affects young adults' communication styles can offer insights into what age groups will choose to communicate.

The comments and preferences of young adults influence the development of AI technology and communication platforms. Developers may uncover opportunities for innovation and improvement by observing users' interactions using AI-powered tools. It will enable the future development of more complex and approachable communication solutions. Communication technologies are fundamental in forming social relationships, norms, and habits.

Studying how AI affects young people's communication patterns might shed light on more general shifts in social dynamics, cultural norms, and organizational structures as they push society reforms. By examining data on the use of AI-powered communication tools by young adults, researchers can spot new patterns and forecast changes in user preferences, market dynamics, and technological acceptance in the future. Investments in AI technology and communication platforms, as well as strategic decision-making, can be informed by this knowledge.

Comprehending how AI technologies impact young adults' communication patterns generates input that guides the creation, advancement, and use of forthcoming AI-driven solutions. Future generations can benefit from more powerful and effective communication tools developers create by considering user input and catering to changing requirements and preferences. Researching how AI affects young individuals' communication practices provides insight into future inclinations and patterns in the use of technology, interpersonal communication, and societal changes. By utilizing this information, businesses may foresee and prepare for the digital age's changing communication landscape.

AI-Driven Analytics

AI-driven analytics systems monitor social media engagement numbers, spot new trends, and forecast viral content. Young adults frequently rely on social media platforms to keep up with peer activities, cultural trends, and current events, where they will pay more attention and time than work. As a result, it impacts the workplace and daily duties. Online networks shape their social identities and behaviors.

AI-powered chatbots and virtual assistants provide young adults with resources, assistance, and emotional support whenever needed. In addition to conventional support networks and counseling services, these digital companions provide a private setting for discussing delicate subjects, getting guidance, and accessing mental health resources. Overall, AI-powered devices have pros and cons, yet the excess time spent on them will eventually affect their work and professional responsibilities.

Identity Formation

The development of one's identity and personal growth occurs throughout the early adult years. Young adults explore their careers, values, beliefs, interests, and goals throughout this developmental period, which helps to shape their sense of self and purpose. AI-powered technologies are crucial to this process because they offer personalized interactions, experiences, and materials that can shape people's identities and decisions. However, the effects of AI on the mental health and overall well-being of young adults warrant careful attention because of the possible risks connected to excessive screen time, social media use, and exposure to AI algorithms that can build adverse side effects on their careers.

AI-powered technology can modify young adults' identities and choices regarding values and preferences by providing them with tailored material and experiences. It is critical to comprehend how AI technologies affect young adults' mental health and general well-being. The impacts of excessive screen time, social media usage, and exposure to AI algorithms, which may alter perceptions and actions, are hazardous for this age group. While AI-powered technologies provide previously unheard-of chances for individualized interactions and experiences, they also present serious risks to young adults' mental health and general well-being. Through an awareness of the possible consequences of excessive screen time, social media use, and exposure to AI algorithms, businesses and stakeholders can endeavor to establish a digital environment that is both balanced and supportive, thereby facilitating the development of healthy identities, fostering resilience, and promoting holistic well-being among young adults between the ages of 18 and 25 through a communication remodel.

Ethical Considerations

Given the long-term effects that this generation of users of AI technology will have on society, regulatory frameworks and ethical issues about data privacy, algorithmic bias, and responsible AI usage must be investigated. Young adults in this age range have distinct tastes, traits, and developmental phases. The 18 to 25 age range is selected to focus on AI-powered technology usage and communication remodeling. Addressing the potential and problems related to integrating AI in all facets of human life requires understanding how they engage with AI technology and communicate.

Intervene the Existing Communication Model

Research techniques are invaluable for expanding knowledge and gaining fresh perspectives in various academic domains (Albert & Csizér, 2022). Furthermore, the study intends to employ the existing communication model to underscore the need for a remodel, and Berlo's SMCR communication model provides the framework for doing so. As mentioned, qualitative research is a robust and insightful methodology to explore the intricacies of human experiences, behaviors, and perceptions (Albert & Csizér, 2022).

Unlike quantitative research, which relies on numerical data and statistical analysis, it focuses on comprehensive, non-numerical data collection. Qualitative research employs interviews, focus groups, and content analysis to provide in-depth insights into a phenomenon's underlying motivations, emotions, and contextual elements (Albert & Csizér, 2022). The approach is particularly beneficial when studying social and cultural phenomena, as it allows for a profound understanding of the subject matter.

David Berlo's SMCR communication model, created in 1960, is a cornerstone of communication theory (Mitchell & Clark, 2022). The model comprises four essential components: Sender, Message, Channel, and Receiver (SMCR). Each element plays a critical role in the communication process. The sender encodes a message transmitted through a selected channel and receives it from the recipient, who then decodes it. The model emphasizes the importance of selecting appropriate communication channels and employing efficient encoding and decoding procedures (Mitchell & Clark, 2022). It is a commonly used framework for evaluating and enhancing communication strategies in communication studies.

Data Collection

Online Zoom interviews were used to obtain information and insights for the study. Interviews are a systematic and realistic method of gathering data. Usually, it comprises a set of inquiries meant to elicit participants' data, viewpoints, experiences, or attitudes. The interview questions used open-ended questions, which enabled young adults to provide detailed, qualitative data for analysis by allowing them to express their ideas, experiences, and opinions in their own words in a given time frame. With this method, researchers can better comprehend the many viewpoints and worries that young adults, ages 18 to 25, have about using AI-powered devices and may investigate possible solutions for any unfavorable effects that might occur.

Data Gathering -Interviews

The plan was to start by locating and enlisting young adults who lived in Torrance, LA County, California, between 18 and 25 years of age. The plan was to reach prospective participants through online audio-only Zoom interviews. To guarantee informed consent was included in the email, all information were sent to the 15 participants by requesting their availability for a Zoom meeting. The email contained details regarding the study's objectives, the interview process, and confidentiality policies. After selecting 15 participants, the researcher connected and worked with them via email to schedule Zoom sessions.

The plan included providing participants with confirmation emails that include the date and time of the online Zoom interview, giving detailed directions on participating in the interview and the time per session, sending reminders closer to the interview date to ensure participants do not forget or skip the planned session, getting familiar with the interview process before the interview and prepare open-ended questions to elicit in-depth and comprehensive answers from the participants, and ensuring the interview questions were pertinent to the study's goals and appropriate for the experiences and viewpoints of young people in Torrance, California, between 18 and 25.

Interview Steps

The researcher used an open-source pre-existing questionnaire as the instrument. As per the questionnaire, the researcher inquired about the participants' usage, frequency experiences, and comprehension of AI-powered devices at work or in the study. The researcher used open-ended questions with the participant's consent to account for the in-depth research methodology used in the study and to provide rich data. Then the researcher recorded the Zoom sessions, transcribed the Zoom conversation via Otter.ai, cleansed raw data, and analyzed constructed data using Python.

Online Zoom interviews were organized at the appointed time and day by extending a warm welcome to the participant and restating the study's objectives and guarantees of anonymity, establishing a welcoming and comfortable space that encourages candid conversation and introspection, and giving the participant enough time to deliberately and thoroughly answer the planned interview questions. To foster more profound knowledge and generate in-depth answers, the participants were encouraged to express their experiences, thoughts, and ideas freely. The researcher may do this by asking clarifying or probing questions as required. The interview was recorded with the participant's permission, and the participant was given a choice to say no if they would rather not be there.

Accurate transcription and analysis of the information acquired during the interview were made possible by recording the session and giving participants a chance to voice any queries or contribute any other insights they may have. If the researcher needs to follow up, reiterate any necessary actions or contact details and ensure that the replies are correctly captured. Transcribe the interview after it has been conducted. Determine themes, patterns, and insight pertinent to the study goals by analyzing the interview data. If the study needed further information or explanations, the participants were contacted. The researcher can efficiently collect qualitative data from young individuals residing in Torrance, California, 18 and 25, through a methodical approach to online Zoom interviews. During data-gathering, this approach respects ethical rules, maintains anonymity, and guarantees flexibility, accessibility, and participant participation.

The Questionnaire

Open access link: https://www.ncbi.nlm.nih.gov/pmc/articles/PMC4338964/

Instrument: Appendix A

Data Analysis

Online Zoom Interviews

Python is the primary analysis tool that analyzes data from an open-ended questionnaire to glean insightful information and make inferences. The study determined valuable insights from the responses of the 15 young adults aged 18 to 25, which involves a systematic approach to analyzing qualitative data obtained from the planned online Zoom interview, particularly those featuring open-ended questions aligned with the study's objectives. The step-by-step process below outlines how to analyze qualitative data from an interview questionnaire, designed to be straightforward and encourage thorough participant responses (Bruckermann et al., 2022). The distribution plan involves disseminating the questionnaire to the target population through emails.

The subsequent focus is on the organization of data. Once all responses were collected, the researcher meticulously organized the information. Spreadsheet programs like Excel can efficiently capture and store responses for analysis (Chennouk et al., 2022). The third step, data cleaning, involved thoroughly reviewing responses to ensure accuracy, comprehensiveness, and the absence of mistakes or contradictions. Duplicate or irrelevant information was deleted, maintaining rigor and transparency throughout the qualitative data analysis. Python tool and its libraries ensured that clear rationales for coding and interpretation decisions were supplied and comprehensive documentation of all conclusions reached during the study was maintained.

The goal was to identify themes and clean significant insights from the open-ended questionnaire, aligning with the research objectives (Chennouk et al., 2022). The next step was data entry and analysis. Following interview completion, the gathered data were entered and examined. Qualitative data analysis methods, such as coding and thematic analysis, were applied to the open-ended questions to uncover and scrutinize noteworthy themes and patterns within the responses.

Assumptions and Delimitations

Assumptions

One presumption was that among the 18 to 25 age range, the participants' technology usage habits were consistent and representative. It was presumed that their answers appropriately represented their interactions with AI-powered devices. The technique was predicated on participants answering the interview questionnaire truthfully and precisely. Their responses were assumed to be sincere and free of prejudice or intentional distortion.

The study's conclusions were anticipated to be applied to a larger group of young adults with comparable demographic traits. It was predicated on the chosen sample sufficiently representing the intended audience. The approach was predicated on the idea that participant reports of the advantages and disadvantages of AI integration fairly represented the real effects of AI-powered technologies on young adults. It presupposed a direct relationship between perceptions and tangible consequences.

Delimitations

Geographical Scope: The research was confined to young adults in a particular geographic area, such as Torrance city in LA County, between the ages of 18 and 25. The results might not apply to other regions with distinct sociocultural backgrounds.

Age Range: Young adults between 18 and 25 were the only age group included in the study; older or younger age groups were excluded. As a result, teenagers or those older than this may not be able to use the findings.

Methodological Approach: An open-ended online Zoom interview was the only tool used in this research. The methodology might potentially restrict the breadth of insights acquired compared to more qualitative techniques like focus groups or surveys.

Time Restrictions: Because the research had a set duration, the scope and depth of data gathering and analysis was limited. Although anonymity was necessary to promote truthful answers, investigating or elucidating participant responses was more complicated. It might limit how deeply the data could be understood. Rather than using objective metrics to gauge the influence of the technology, the study focused on participants' opinions about AI-powered devices in their careers and general ideas about AI and business. It restricted the study's focus to personal opinions and might not adequately account for all of technology's consequences.

Trustworthiness

A specific emphasis was placed on the thorough training and calibration of observers to ensure the reliability of the data. Before the commencement of the study, the targeted audience were sent a document about the research study, its goals, the reason for selecting the particular target group, and data protection criteria. In that manner, the targeted group familiarized themselves with the research goals, ethical considerations, and standard operating procedures. Calibration activities such as consistency check, reflexivity, or member checking were conducted to minimize potential bias and ensure consistency in data collection.

Reflexivity and researcher positionality were actively incorporated to address the possible impact of researcher subjectivity on the data (B. Lee et al., 2022). Scholars consistently reflected on their viewpoints, past experiences, and any prejudices that might influence the findings. Regular debriefing meetings addressed biases or assumptions that may surface and foster a more nuanced interpretation of the gathered information (B. Lee et al., 2022). Triangulation involving the cross-referencing and evaluation of various data sources, such as targeted questionnaire results and pre-existing demographic information, were employed to enhance the reliability and validity of the results. Its multifaceted approach ensured a more thorough and accurate portrayal of the dynamics and behaviors of young adults in Los Angeles County.

The research concept, methods, and findings underwent a thorough peer review to enhance the study's credibility. Colleagues and subject-matter specialists were invited to assess the work and provide critical, insightful commentary. The external examination serves to validate the results of the research (B. Lee et al., 2022). The research aimed to maintain the highest levels of reliability in gathering and processing data, ensuring that the results appropriately represent the interactions and behaviors of young adults in Los Angeles County.

Summary

The study delved into the perspectives and insights of young individuals aged 18 to 25 in Torrance, California, regarding the 'Future Implications of AI-Powered Technology on Young Adults: The Need for a Revised Communication Model.' To comprehensively grasp the attitudes, behaviors, and experiences of this target demographic, the researcher employed a qualitative research methodology: an open-ended questionnaire. The approach offered a comprehensive understanding of how AI technology and associated communication models impact the lives of young adults.

The study described how the online Zoom interview with an open-ended questionnaire method systematically collects self-reported data, enabling participants to express their thoughts in detail and offer responses scrutinized for recurring patterns and themes. By employing an open-ended questionnaire for the interview, the study was well-positioned to provide a holistic view of how young adults perceive the potential implications of AI technology and the necessity for updated communication paradigms. The insights gained will contribute to a better understanding of how AI technology and communication strategies shape the lives of young adults aged 18 to 25.

CHAPTER FOUR: RESULTS

The chapter reiterates the research questions (RQs) and their corresponding interview responses. This is followed by a description of the participants aged 18 to 25 who reside in Torrance, California. These individuals either have a professional background, have recently completed their higher studies, are awaiting the start of their careers, or have just begun their careers. The chapter details how their thoughts and experiences were represented in the sample through audio-only interviews conducted via Zoom, providing a comprehensive overview of their perspectives and insights relevant to the study.

The interviews were conducted via Zoom—Inc., with audio recordings saved on the researcher's computer with password protection. The participants' identities will remain anonymous and confidential during and after the study. Only the researcher will have access to the data. According to University guidelines, the Zoom conversation will be deleted from the researcher's computer after 3 years. To maintain the confidentiality of the participants, they have asked to refrain from placing their names or any other identifying information on any research form or protocol.

All recorded information will be securely stored for 3 years per Westcliff University requirements, after which all data will be deleted, and all written data will be shredded. The records of this study will be kept private, with no identifiers linking to the survey included in any published report. The audio files were transcribed using the Otter.ai tool and stored in separate folders for each participant. All participant files were imported into Python.Org, the programming language tool for data analysis, where each question and sub-question, participants' responses, and frequently used keywords were coded and labeled. These codes were used to identify participants, research topics, relevant interview questions posed by the interviewer, and responses given by the interviewees.

In this chapter, the researcher brought the research questions, participant responses, codes, findings, results, and analysis, ending with a summary of the overall study. This comprehensive approach ensured that each aspect of the research was thoroughly examined. The chapter aimed to clearly and concisely understand the study's outcomes and implications.

Data Collection

The data for this study were gathered through recorded audio Zoom interviews involving the researcher as the interviewer and 15 interviewees. The steps involved in the data collection procedure were as follows:

- The initial post went live on the social media platform 'WhatsApp.'
- Collected the emails from the respondents who are interested in participating in the study through the initial post
- Sent out the IRB-approved invitation email to those who showed interest
- Sent out an approved follow-up email with the consent letter to be signed and requesting a convenient date and time for the Zoom interview
- Sent out an email with the Zoom invitation link
- Attended Zoom interviews with each interested participant separately and recorded each session
- Saved Zoom recordings and transcripts generated through Otter.ai and manually cleansed data in the researcher's personal computer with password protection.
- Installed Python.org and its libraries

- Generated codes and keywords through NLTK and executed each query to generate results
- Converted results into visualization through Matplotlib

Appendix A provides the list of questions, and Appendix B contains the raw data of the interview transcripts.

Nature of the Questions in the Interview

The researcher utilized a preexisting closed-ended questionnaire, The Media and Technology Usage and Attitudes Scale: An Empirical Investigation (Rosen et al., 2013). This is an open-access article, and the link to the article is:

https://www.ncbi.nlm.nih.gov/pmc/articles/PMC4338964/

Instrument: Appendix A

Data Collection Through Interviews

The information gathered was considered unique and uniform regarding 'The Future Implications of AI-powered Technology on Young Adults: The Need for a Revised Communication Model. The 15 participants were aged 18 to 25 and reside in Torrance, California. These individuals either have a professional background, have recently completed their higher studies, are awaiting the start of their careers, or have just begun their careers. The researcher conducted the Zoom audio-only interview to get the responses from these 15 participants.

Characteristics of the Participants

The researcher recruited the participants through a social media platform, WhatsApp group, and only targeted young adults aged 18 to 25 living in Torrance, California. Survey participants have either completed their education and are seeking a career, professional guidance, and path or have recently joined a career. Other than allowing the researcher to carry out the study, the organizations these young adults work for, or any educational institute, had no further involvement in the procedure.

Results of Data Collection

The data-gathering findings included the format of the recordings and the transcription process for the audio files. The following subsections provide descriptions of these specifics. This detailed breakdown will offer insights into the methodological choices made during the study. Understanding these aspects is crucial for interpreting the accuracy and reliability of the collected data.

Zoom Recorded Audio Files. The replies to the questions from the qualitative interview were recorded using a Zoom conference in which the participant and the researcher connected using their devices. The discussion was captured on audio without any discrepancy and stored on the researcher's desktop PC. The snapshot of each participant's audio and text transcriptions is displayed in Figure 1.

Figure 1

Screenshot of Audio and Text Files of a Participant from the Interview

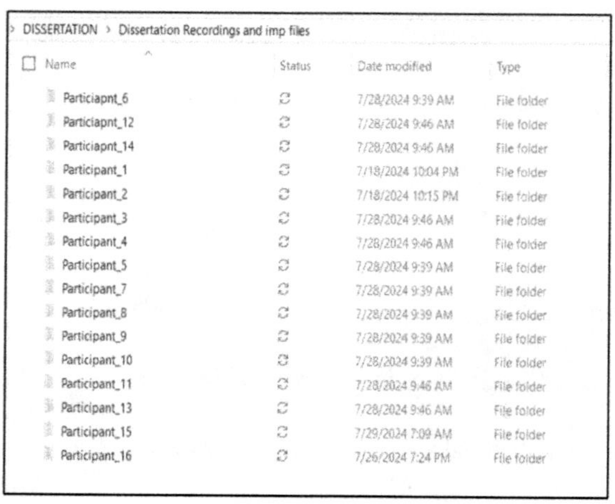

Figure 2

Screenshot of Audio and Text Files of a Participant from the Interview

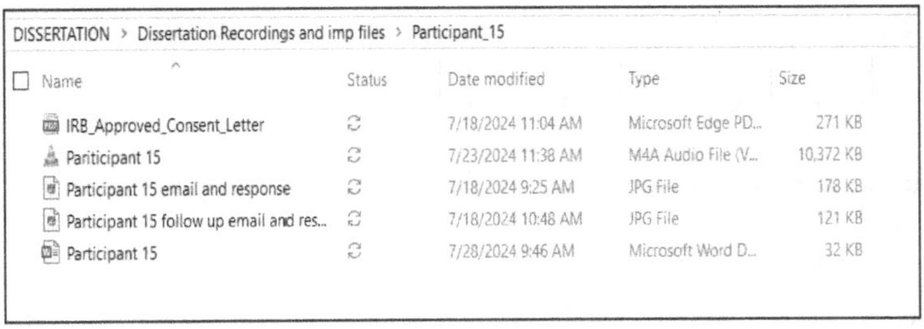

Audio File Transcription. The audio files were imported using the internet resources provided by the otter.ai transcription service (www.otter.ai). After the audio recordings were loaded into the web application, each transcription was completed independently and stored in its folder. The web tools' snapshot displaying the transcription for one of the participant's audios is shown below.

Figure 3

Screenshot of a Transcription Processed for one Participant

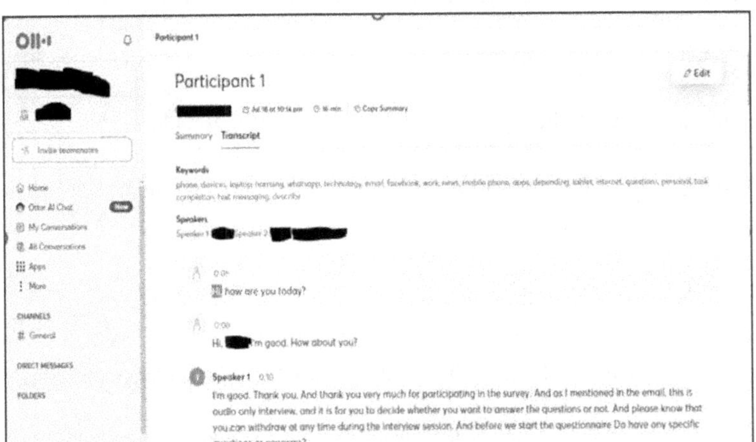

Appendix B contains all 15 interview transcripts in their entirety. The transcripts' headers correspond to the subjects of the interview. For instance, the transcript of Interview 1. is available in Appendix B.1. The transcript of Interview 2 is available in Appendix B.2. Likewise, Appendix B.15 contains the transcript of Interview 15. These transcripts show that the Otter.ai service could only distinguish between two distinct speakers. The first person to speak was named Participant 1, and the second was named Participant 2.

Data Analysis Using Python as a Computer-Assisted Qualitative Data Analysis Software

The researcher employed Python.org to analyze audio recordings and interview transcripts due to its extensive libraries and tools, making it a popular choice for quantitative and qualitative data analysis (Srinath, 2017). Responses from 15 participants were collected. These responses are stored in a structured format, a JSON format.

Text Analysis and Processing: Two powerful libraries for NLP (NLP) in Python are spaCy and NLTK (Natural Language Toolkit). These libraries assist with tokenization, stemming, lemmatization, and other text preparation activities. TextBlob is another tool used for text analysis, enabling sentiment analysis and noun phrase extraction (Lutz, 2010).

Theme and Pattern Identification: The researcher used Python to identify themes and patterns in the collected data—topic modeling, particularly with Latent Dirichlet Allocation (LDA), which effectively conducted library Gensim. Gensim offers various tools and functions for working with text data, including topic modeling, word embedding, and document similarity (Lutz, 2010).

Data Preparation Steps

- Installation: The researcher installed Python along with the necessary libraries.
- Cleaning and Preprocessing: The text data were cleaned and preprocessed, including tokenization, removing stopwords, and lemmatization.

- Dictionary Creation: The corpus was converted into a dictionary of unique words and their corresponding IDs.
- Corpus Representation: Documents in the corpus were represented in a bag-of-words or term frequency-inverse document frequency (TF-IDF) format.
- Topic Exploration: The resulting topics were analyzed, focusing on the most significant words for each topic and the distribution of topics within each document.
- Visualization: The tool pyLDAvis was optionally used to visualize the topics and their relationships.

Qualitative Data Coding: The researcher used Python to write custom coding routines that facilitated systematic organization and classification of qualitative data.

Illustration and Visualization: Visualizations of qualitative data, such as word clouds or frequency distributions, were created using Matplotlib to aid in interpreting and presenting results. Pandas were used for data preparation and cleaning, ensuring the qualitative data were well-organized before analysis (Srinath, 2017).

Creation of Project File and Importing all the Project Supporting Documents

The Python program imported all 15 papers into a new project file. The project file had the following imported documents:

- 15 interview transcripts
- 15 audio recordings of the conversations
- The file contains the collection of study questions and subquestions.

Following the import of all required documents, the coding process was started to analyze qualitative data.

Data Coding Procedures

As described in Chapter Three of the methodology, coding was performed on the transcripts to examine the data by identifying themes and codes in segments and assigning portions of the material to respective codes. Codes are considered tags or labels that assign meaning to units of data (Srinath, 2017). These codes can be applied to chunks of various sizes, such as individual words, phrases, sentences, or entire paragraphs. Coding serves as a data management method that also aids in analysis.

In the study, the researcher differentiated between themes and codes. The researcher defines codes as concise labels highlighting areas of interest within the data. At the same time, themes are broader ideas or concepts that form regular, recurring patterns across a dataset and focus on a primary organizing concept (Srinath, 2017).

Coding the Participants of the Interviews. The initial step in building the code was to generate codes for each speaker in each transcript. Using the auto coding feature in the software, replacing "Participant 1" and "Participant 2" with the actual individuals being interviewed was possible. In the transcripts, only "Participant" and "Participant 2" were named, with "Participant 1" typically being the one who started the conversation.

In most transcripts, the interviewee was labeled "Participant 1" and the researcher "Participant 2." However, in some transcripts, this designation was reversed, with the researcher as "Participant 1" and the interviewee as "Participant 2." To prevent these errors, a code that identifies the researcher and the interviewee must be included in each transcript.

Table 1

Codes of the Participants

Interview Number	Interviewer Code	Interviewee Code
Interview 1	RQ	P1
Interview 2	RQ	P2
Interview 3	RQ	P3
Interview 4	RQ	P4
Interview 5	RQ	P5
Interview 6	RQ	P6
Interview 7	RQ	P7
Interview 8	RQ	P8
Interview 9	RQ	P9
Interview 10	RQ	P10
Interview 11	RQ	P11
Interview 12	RQ	P12
Interview 13	RQ	P13
Interview 14	RQ	P14
Interview 15	RQ	P15

As seen in Table 1, the researcher was Speaker 1, and the participants were shown as P1, P2, and P3 until P15, which is recognized as Speaker 2.

Codes for the Research Questions and Sub Questions. The codes established for the research questions and sub-questions are listed below. The researcher (Speaker 1), identified as 6

Research Questions (RQ), formulated and posed these questions and sub-questions. All the questions listed below received approval from the IRB.

Table 2

Codes of the Research Questions and Sub Questions

SNO	Interview Questions	Code
1	How often do you use email services on any smart device, such as a mobile phone, laptop, desktop, etc., for your personal, work, or school/university life, and for what purpose?	RQ1
2	Can you briefly explain how you differentiate the use of devices regarding personal, work, or school emails?	RQ1.1
3	Describe your daily use of text messaging and phone calls.	RQ2
4	How do you use your mobile phone for internet activities and apps?	RQ2.1
5	What are your primary reasons for using GPS, music, and media on your phone?	RQ2.2
6	How does your mobile phone usage differ during work or class?	RQ2.3
7	How do you consume TV shows, movies, and video clips across different devices?	RQ3
8	Describe your habits around downloading and sharing media files.	RQ3.1
9	How do you use the Internet for news, information, and entertainment?	RQ3.2
10	How do you engage with social networking sites like Facebook?	RQ4
11	What is your posting, commenting, and liking content habits?	RQ4.1

SNO	Interview Questions	Code
12	How many online friends do you know in person versus online?	RQ4.2
13	How important is it for you to access information and the Internet anytime?	RQ5
14	How do you keep up with the latest technology trends?	RQ5.1
15	In what ways do you believe technology solves problems or complicates life?	RQ5.2
16	Describe any anxiety or dependence you feel regarding technology.	RQ5.3
17	How do you simultaneously manage multiple tasks or assignments on any device (mobile phone, laptop, desktop, etc.)?	RQ6
18	What is your approach to task completion and intermittent switching on those devices?	RQ6.1

Codes for the Responses to the Interview Questions. The responses to each interview question were coded using Python coding to generate the codes, which were then applied to all answers for each question and sub-question. Each participant's responses were grouped under a single code created by the software. The researcher maps responses to codes and then applies a text-processing method to generate unique codes.

Complete Code Example

- Import necessary libraries: import pandas as pd and hashlib
- Define the DataFrame
- Function to generate hash codes
- Generate codes for all 15 responses

- Display the data frame with codes

Following these steps, the researcher generates a data frame where a unique code accompanies each response.

Analysis of Interview Responses

Figure 4

Top 20 Device Usage Purposes

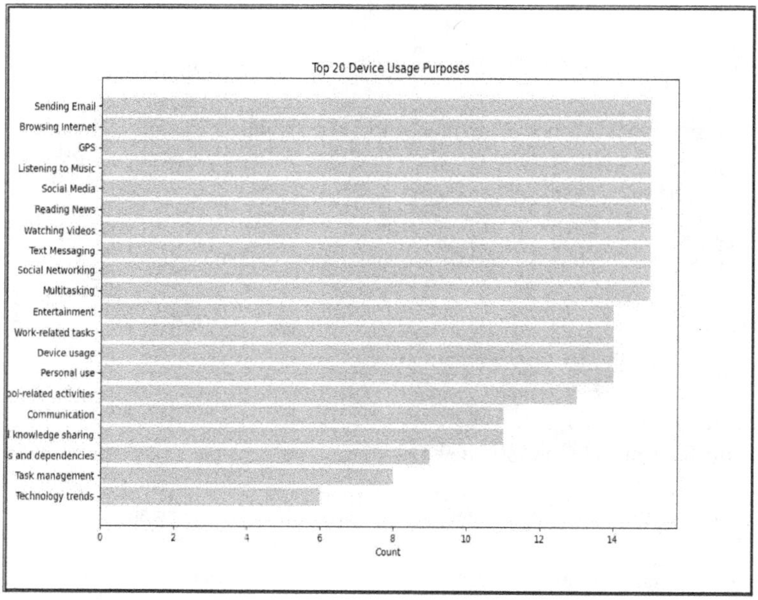

The chart effectively captures the 15 participants' broad range of device usage purposes. It highlights common trends in how devices are integral to daily tasks, both professional and personal.

Key Insights and Analysis

Top Usage Purposes: The chart lists the top 20 purposes for the 15 participants using their devices. Each purpose is represented by a bar, and the length of the bar indicates the number of participants who mentioned that particular usage.

Uniformity in Usage: The most frequently mentioned usage purposes are consistent across all 15 participants, such as "Sending Email," "Browsing the Internet," "GPS," "Listening to Music," "Social Media," "Reading News," "Watching Videos," "Text Messaging," "Social Networking," and "Multitasking." These bars are fully extended, indicating that all participants use their devices for these purposes.

Variation in Usage: There is some variation in less common usage purposes, such as "Entertainment," "Work-related tasks," "Device usage," "Personal use," "School-related activities," "Communication," "Information and knowledge sharing," "Managing distractions and dependencies," "Task management," and "Technology trends." These purposes have shorter bars, indicating that fewer participants mentioned them.

Insights on Device Dependence: High Dependence on Common Tasks: Activities like emailing, internet browsing, and GPS navigation are universally important, as all participants use their devices for these tasks. Entertainment and Social Media: These are also significant usage purposes, reflecting the dual role of devices in work and leisure.

Importance of Device Usage in Daily Life: Multitasking: The high frequency indicates that participants often use their devices to handle multiple tasks simultaneously. Work and Personal Use: The differentiation between work-related and personal use shows devices' versatility in managing different aspects of participants' lives. School-related Activities: For those participants engaged in academic pursuits, devices are crucial for school-related tasks.

Comparative Insights: Homogeneous Usage: The top 10 purposes are almost uniformly used by all participants, highlighting standard device usage patterns. Heterogeneous Usage: The lower-ranked purposes exhibit more variation, suggesting that while some uses are universal, others are more specialized or personal.

Technology Trends and Task Management: Emerging Trends: Following technology trends is less common but still significant, indicating a proactive approach among some participants to stay updated with technological advancements. Task Management: Using devices to manage tasks and information underscores their role in enhancing productivity and organization.

The figure illustrates the diverse range of purposes for which the 15 participants use their devices. It underscores prevalent trends, showcasing how these devices are essential in both professional and personal daily tasks. Additionally, the chart reveals insights into specific device usage patterns, highlighting the integral nature of technology in managing day-to-day activities, improving productivity, and enhancing personal convenience. The uniformity in specific high-frequency tasks underscores their universal importance, while the variation in other tasks suggests more personalized or context-specific usage patterns. This analysis provides a comprehensive overview of how participants interact with their devices and the critical roles these devices play in their lives.

Figure 5

Preferred Devices for Communication Among Participants

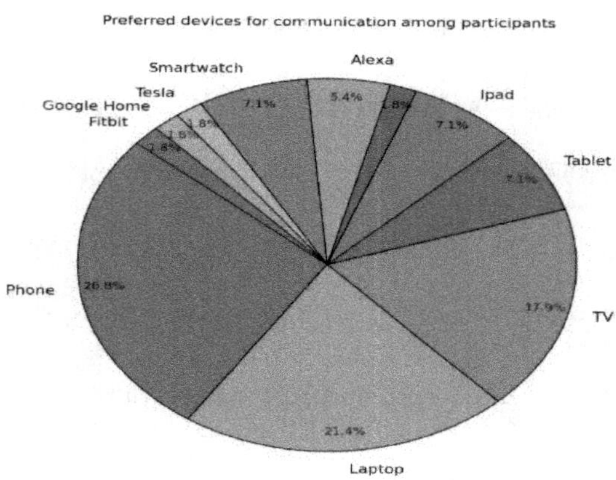

The pie chart illustrates the preferred communication devices among 15 participants based on their responses during the Zoom interview.

Key Insights and Analysis

Phone (26.8%): The phone is the most preferred device for communication among participants, with 26.8% indicating it as their primary choice. This preference is likely due to the phone's versatility, portability, and the wide range of communication applications it supports, such as calling, texting, and various messaging apps.

Laptop (21.4%): Laptops are the second most preferred device at 21.4%. This choice is probably due to the larger screen size, keyboard, and the ability to handle more complex tasks such as emails, video conferencing, and document editing, which are essential for work and education.

TV (17.9%): TVs, used by 17.9% of participants, may seem like an unusual choice for communication. However, smart TVs now support apps like Skype, Zoom, and other video conferencing tools, making them a viable option for home-based communication, especially for video calls.

Tablet (7.1%): Tablets are used by 7.1% of participants. They balance the portability of a phone and the larger screen size of a laptop, making them suitable for casual communication and more intensive tasks.

iPad (7.1%): Similar to tablets, the iPad is also preferred by 7.1% of participants. With its robust ecosystem and powerful apps, the iPad provides a seamless experience for communication and other tasks.

Alexa (5.4%): Alexa is used by 5.4% of participants. As a smart home assistant, Alexa can facilitate communication through voice commands, making calls, sending messages, and even video calls via compatible devices.

Smartwatch (1.8%): Only 1.8% of participants prefer using a smartwatch. While smartwatches are primarily used for quick notifications and brief communications, their smaller screen size and limited functionality may restrict their use for more detailed communication tasks.

Tesla (1.8%): Interestingly, 1.8% of participants use Tesla as an autonomous car that operates entirely through software. Modern cars come with advanced infotainment systems that support hands-free calls and voice commands, providing a convenient option for communication while driving.

Google Home (1.8%): Google Home is also preferred by 1.8% of participants. Like Alexa, Google Home offers voice-activated communication features, including calls and messaging.

Fitbit (1.8%): Fitbit, used by 1.8% of participants, is primarily a fitness tracker, but some models offer basic communication features like call and text notifications.

The figure indicates various preferred communication devices, reflecting the participants' varied needs and contexts. The dominance of phones and laptops suggests that these devices are essential for their portability, functionality, and versatility. This variety highlights the importance of device choice in communication, driven by specific user needs and situational contexts. The preference for smart devices like phones and laptops emphasizes their continued relevance and reliability in everyday communication.

Figure 6

Communication Methods Among Participants

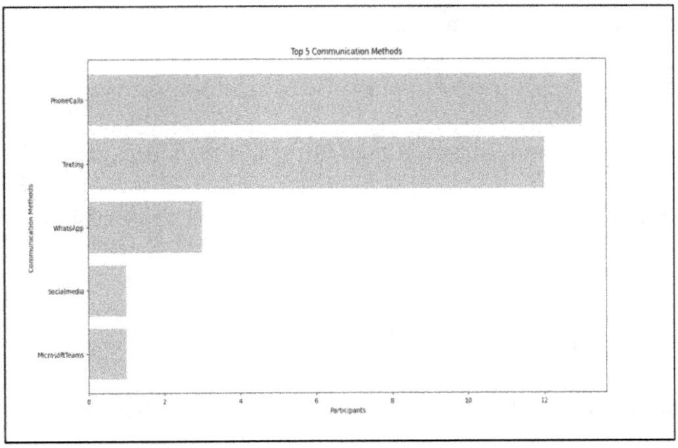

This bar chart displays the frequency of participants' most common communication methods. The x-axis represents the different communication methods, while the y-axis shows the frequency of participants using each method.

Key Insights and Analysis

Phone Calls: Participants' most frequently used communication method. This indicates that phone calls are highly valued for their immediacy and the ability to convey tone and emotion effectively. In professional and personal settings, phone calls provide a direct and personal means of communication, which can be critical for nuanced conversations or urgent matters.

Texting: Texting is the second most common communication method. Texting's high frequency suggests it is a convenient and efficient communication method, especially for short messages or when real-time conversation is unnecessary. Text's brevity and asynchronous nature make it ideal for quick updates and casual communication.

WhatsApp: WhatsApp is a significant communication method among participants. WhatsApp's popularity can be attributed to its features like group messaging, multimedia sharing, and cross-platform functionality. It is widely used for personal and group communications, allowing for rich interaction beyond simple text.

Social Media: Social media is less frequently used than the top three methods, but it is still notable. Social media platforms (e.g., Facebook, Twitter, and LinkedIn) serve broader communication purposes, including networking, information sharing, and public engagement. The less frequent use of direct communication might be due to these platforms' being more public and less immediate.

Microsoft Teams: Microsoft Teams is used less frequently than the other methods. Microsoft Teams is primarily a professional communication tool widely used in corporate and educational settings for collaboration and meetings. Its lower frequency might reflect its specific use case compared to general communication tools like phone calls and texting.

Figure 7

Positive and Negative Attitudes Towards Technology

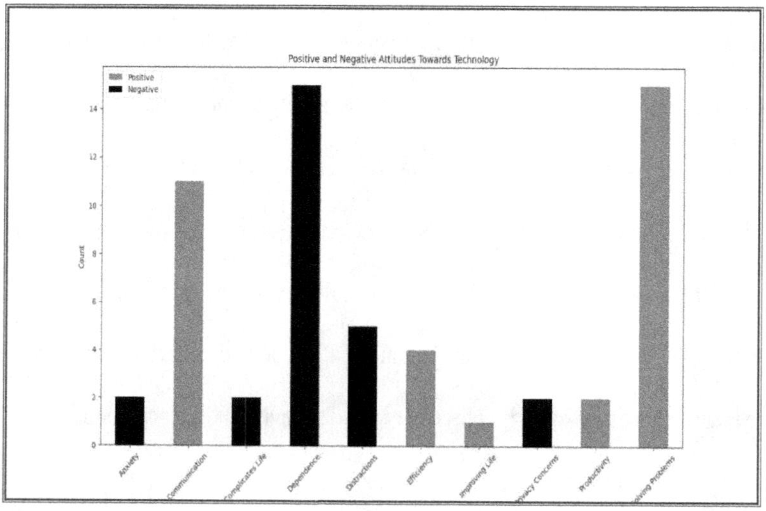

This visualization is a stacked bar chart representing the positive and negative attitudes toward technology among 15 participants, depending on their responses.

Key Insights and Analysis

Dependence: This is the most frequently mentioned negative attitude, indicating that many participants feel that technology creates a sense of dependency.

Communication: This is the most frequently mentioned positive attitude, suggesting that technology is highly valued for improving communication.

Solving Problems: This is another prominent positive attitude, highlighting the perception that technology helps solve problems.

Distractions: This is a significant negative attitude, showing that technology can be a source of distractions.

Efficiency and Productivity: These are critical positive attitudes, indicating that technology is seen as a tool for improving efficiency and productivity.

Complicates Life and Privacy Concerns: These negative attitudes are less frequently mentioned but still notable, reflecting concerns about how technology can complicate life and raise privacy issues.

This stacked bar chart visualization provides a clear and comparative view of the participants' positive and negative attitudes toward technology. Using Python tools such as Pandas and Matplotlib, the researcher processed the data effectively and created an informative visual representation. The stacked bar chart lets the reader see the balance between positive and negative attitudes and identify the most commonly mentioned sentiments.

Figure 8

Impact of Device Usage on Work (Top 20 Purposes)

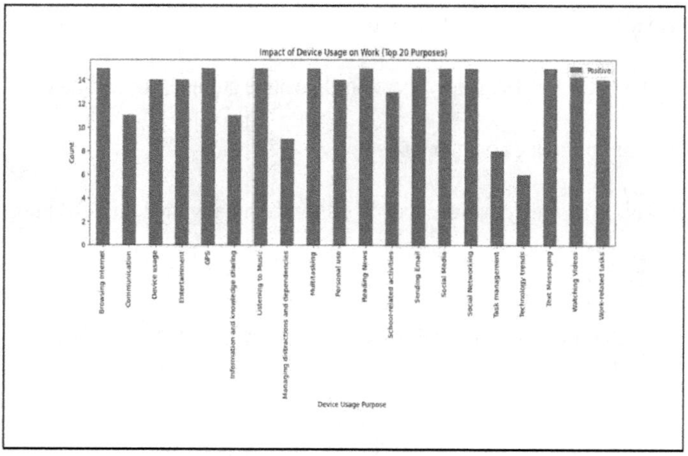

This bar chart illustrates the impact of device usage on work for the top 20 purposes as reported by participants. Each bar represents a specific purpose, and the height indicates the frequency with which participants perceive this purpose positively impacting their work.

Key Insights and Analysis

Positive Impact: All the top 20 device usage purposes are reported to impact work positively. This indicates that participants find these activities to enhance their work performance or work-related outcomes.

High-Frequency Purposes:

- Browsing Internet: This is one of the purposes with the highest frequency. It likely includes activities such as researching information, accessing online tools, and using cloud-based services, which can significantly boost productivity.
- Listening to Music: Many participants find that listening to music while working helps improve concentration, reduce stress, and increase overall productivity.

- Sending Email: This is another high-frequency purpose. Email remains a crucial tool for professional communication, enabling quick exchange of information, coordination, and collaboration.

Other Notable Purposes:

- Reading News: Keeping updated with current events can be essential for staying informed and making better decisions in a professional context.
- Multitasking: The ability to use devices for multitasking is highly valued, indicating that participants appreciate the efficiency gains from handling multiple tasks simultaneously.
- Social Networking: Platforms like LinkedIn can be valuable for professional networking, finding job opportunities, and keeping in touch with industry trends.

Summary of Findings

The study involved 15 participants aged 18 to 25 residing in Torrance, California. These participants were professionals, recent graduates, or individuals awaiting the start of their careers. The data were collected through audio-only Zoom interviews, ensuring the anonymity and confidentiality of participants.

Data Collection and Analysis

Data Collection: Zoom audio interviews were conducted, recorded, and transcribed using Otter.ai. The data were securely stored and later analyzed using Python.

Data Analysis: The transcripts were imported into Python, where NLP (NLP) tools like spaCy and NLTK were used for text analysis. Themes and patterns were identified using topic modeling with Gensim. Visualizations were created using Matplotlib.

Device Usage Purposes

- Top Purposes: The most common device usage purposes included sending emails, browsing the Internet, using GPS, listening to music, engaging with social media, reading news, watching videos, and multitasking.
- Device Dependence: High dependence was noted on everyday tasks such as emailing, internet browsing, and GPS navigation, highlighting the integral role of devices in daily life.

Preferred Communication Devices

- Top Devices: Phones and laptops were the most preferred communication devices, followed by TVs, tablets, iPads, and smart home assistants like Alexa and Google Home. These preferences reflect the versatility and functionality of these devices in facilitating communication.

Communication Methods

- Standard Methods: Phone calls, texting, and WhatsApp were the most frequently used communication methods. Social media and Microsoft Teams were also used, but less frequently.
- Usage Contexts: The choice of communication method varied based on the context, with phone calls being preferred for direct and personal conversations and texting for quick updates.

Attitudes Toward Technology

- Positive Attitudes: Participants highlighted the benefits of technology in improving communication, solving problems, and enhancing efficiency and productivity.

- Negative Attitudes: Concerns about dependence on technology, distractions, and privacy issues were raised.

Impact of Device Usage on Work

- Positive Impacts: Participants reported that device usage positively impacted their work, mainly through activities like browsing the Internet, listening to music, and sending emails. These activities were associated with increased productivity and better work outcomes.
- Multitasking: The ability to multitask using devices was highly valued, indicating that participants often handled multiple tasks simultaneously, enhancing their overall productivity.

Summary

The study provides comprehensive insights into the device usage patterns, communication preferences, and attitudes toward technology among young adults in Torrance, California. The findings highlight the essential role of technology in both professional and personal contexts, underscoring the need for a balanced approach to managing its benefits and challenges.

CHAPTER FIVE: CONCLUSIONS

The study provides comprehensive insights into device usage patterns, communication preferences, and attitudes toward technology among young adults in Torrance, California. The participants include individuals with varying professional backgrounds: those who have recently completed their higher studies, are awaiting the start of their careers, or have just begun their professional journey. The chapter describes how their perspectives were captured through audio-only interviews conducted via Zoom, offering a detailed overview of their experiences and insights.

This chapter delves into a comprehensive analysis of the findings from Chapter Four, interpreting the implications of these results, discussing the study's limitations, exploring its transferability, and providing detailed recommendations for future research and practical applications. The insights gained from this study contribute to the broader understanding of the role of AI-powered technology in shaping young adults' communication habits and productivity.

The findings of Chapter Four underscore the crucial role of technology in both personal and professional contexts, emphasizing the need for a balanced approach to leveraging its benefits while managing its challenges. The results suggest that young adults aged 18 to 25 effectively manage their AI-powered device usage during work, which has not negatively impacted their professional performance. However, the analysis indicates that introducing a communication remodel, such as Berlo's SMCR Model, could enhance the efficiency and effectiveness of communication among young adults. This adjustment is recommended to further optimize the use of AI-powered technology in their daily personal, professional, and academic activities, ensuring that communication practices are aligned with the evolving technological landscape.

Interpretations and Implications

Overview of the Results

The study focused on 15 participants aged 18 to 25 residing in Torrance, California, representing a range of educational and professional backgrounds. Data were collected through audio-only Zoom interviews, a method chosen for its convenience and ability to maintain participant anonymity. The interviews were transcribed and analyzed using Python's advanced NLP (NLP) tools, which enabled a thorough exploration of the participants' responses.

Device Usage Purposes

Email and Internet Browsing. The study revealed that sending emails and browsing the internet are among the most frequent activities for participants, reflecting their reliance on these tools for personal and professional tasks. This finding underscores the centrality of these digital activities in daily life.

Participant 1 mentioned, "I use emails daily for work, personal, and university purposes. For work, I use my laptop specifically. I use my mobile phone for personal and university matters because it has all the apps I need and is very convenient."

Participant 2 mentioned,

> I use emails daily for work and personal use. I check my emails on my phone and always use my work computer for work emails. This helps me keep my personal and work communications separate. For school emails, I use my personal computer. This way, each type of email is managed on a specific device.

Participant 6 replied,

> I use email almost all the time for work and personal purposes. I prefer using laptops for most tasks to avoid using iPhones and iPads. Due to my job in IT, I primarily use email

for work-related communication. I use personal email to manage my stock portfolio and search for real estate properties. I spend about five to six hours a day monitoring and responding to emails.

GPS and Music. GPS usage indicates the participants' reliance on technology for navigation while listening to music during tasks, highlighting technology's role in managing personal well-being and productivity.

Participant 5 replied, "GPS is essential because I travel frequently and need navigation assistance. I use music for entertainment and relaxation. Media usage on my phone is mainly for entertainment when I have spare time."

Participant 8 replied, "GPS is essential for navigating to new places. Music is for relaxation, especially during travel or workouts. Media, like videos and social media, is for entertainment and staying connected with friends and family."

Social Media and Multitasking. The frequent use of social media and the ability to multitask underscore the versatility of modern devices in facilitating a range of activities, from social interaction to efficient task management.

Participant 9 mentioned,

> I actively engage in social media platforms like Facebook, Instagram, TikTok, WhatsApp, and Snapchat. I make friends, follow pages of interest, and join groups related to hobbies or communities. I share personal milestones, photos, and life events, respond to invitations, and check upcoming events.
>
> I use separate devices for work-related tasks to avoid confusion. I take customer calls on my mobile phone, work on customer requirements on my laptop, and use iPads to insert data, ensuring tasks do not get mixed up. I keep Alexa as a side support to remind me of

certain times, and I use a smartwatch for reminders. I switch between tasks to maintain momentum but rely on all devices simultaneously for my work.

Participant 14 said,

I rarely use Facebook or Instagram to post. I spend more time on LinkedIn for professional networking and reading work-related articles. I engage with posts by liking and occasionally commenting, mainly on LinkedIn and Reddit. I manage multiple tasks by splitting them into smaller chunks and using different devices for different tasks. I make to-do lists and switch between devices as needed to complete tasks efficiently.

Effective task management is crucial for participants, who often use productivity apps, to-do lists, and specific devices to organize their work. The preference for laptops and desktops for complex tasks and using mobile phones for quick updates reflects a strategic approach to multitasking. This highlights the need for tools and workflows that support seamless switching between devices and tasks, ensuring productivity without overwhelming the user.

Preferred Communication Devices

Phones and Laptops. The preference for mobile phones and laptops illustrates their indispensable role in modern communication, valued for their portability, functionality, and integration with various applications.

Participant 7 replied,

I use my mobile phone for quick checks and immediate responses. I use a laptop or desktop for detailed responses or to include attachments. I use email for personal purposes, such as communicating with friends, managing subscriptions, and receiving newsletters. I use email for work and university to upgrade assignments, communicate with professors, and schedule meetings.

On my mobile phone, I set reminders and schedule tasks using calendar apps. I keep quick notes and to-do lists in apps like Google Keep. I use task and time management tools and multiple monitors on my laptop or desktop to track different tasks and projects.

Participant 9 replied,

I use my mobile phone for personal, casual, and on-the-go communication. For work, it is for client documentation, advertisements, updates, notifications, and urgent responses. For my laptop or desktop, personal use involves managing personal records, detailed communication, and organizing information.

Smart Devices. Smart home assistants, tablets, and iPads reflect a trend toward integrating technology into various aspects of life, enabling more seamless and efficient communication.

Participant 7 mentioned,

For TV shows and movies, I prefer watching on TV with family or friends due to the larger screen and better audio. I use streaming services directly on the TV. I prefer using a laptop or tablet with services like Netflix to watch movies. For video clips, I use my smartphone to watch YouTube and short video clips.

Participant 9 replied,

I use my phone for short video clips, YouTube videos, and streaming shows during commutes or breaks. Social media platforms like Instagram or Facebook for watching shared videos. For movies and TV shows, I prefer my desktop or laptop for better resolution and quality.

Communication Methods

Phone Calls and Texting. These remain dominant methods of communication, with participants valuing the immediacy and directness of phone calls and the convenience of texting for quick exchanges.

Participant 1 mentioned, "I get many phone calls for work, personal matters, and university-related issues, including calls from university friends. I mainly use WhatsApp for text messaging across all areas of my life-work, personal, and university."

Participant 2 said,

> These days, I do not text much since I use social media and WhatsApp for messaging. I get a few personal calls daily and some work-related calls. I handle personal calls on my phone and work calls on the relevant device as needed.

WhatsApp and Social Media. The popularity of WhatsApp highlights the shift toward messaging apps that offer rich features such as group chats and multimedia sharing. Social media's role, though secondary, is significant in broader communication contexts, including networking and public engagement.

Participant 2 said, "I use Facebook, Instagram, and Snapchat to watch entertaining videos and connect with old friends. I use these platforms to chat and video call."

Participant 4 replied, "I used to use social media like Facebook and Instagram a lot but have since deleted these apps to avoid wasting time. I have not used these platforms for years."

Engagement with social media varies widely among participants. Some are passive users, focusing on liking and occasionally commenting on content, while others are more active, posting updates and engaging in discussions. This variation suggests that social media is used differently depending on individual preferences, with some using it primarily for keeping up with friends and trends, while others use it more selectively for professional networking or specific interests.

Attitudes Toward Technology

Participant 1 mentioned that technology can solve many problems and make life easier if used to its full potential without harming others. However, it can complicate life if it leads to neglecting personal relationships or responsibilities. Participant 1 stated,

> So, it is a 50-50 situation, depending on how it is used. I depend on technology for important information, staying in touch with long-distance relationships, and connecting with friends and family I rarely see. It is crucial for maintaining connections.

Participant 2 replied that technology solves many current problems and has the potential to benefit humans in the long run. However, it can complicate life by creating competition and challenges that require constant learning and adaptation. Participant 2 stated, "There is anxiety about losing jobs to machines and technology. Only those who understand and adapt to technology will thrive as technology advances, potentially replacing many workers."

Participant 3 said technology solves problems by increasing efficiency, streamlining tasks, and enhancing productivity through automation and tools. Participant 3 stated,

> It improves communication and connectivity through instant messaging, video calls, and social media. Technology provides immediate access to vast information and resources and enhances healthcare through telemedicine, health tracking, and advanced medical technologies. However, it complicates life by creating dependency, security concerns, and anxiety over personal data and potential cyber threats. I experience a fear of missing out and worrying about missing important updates, messages, or trends. I have security

concerns about personal data and potential cyber threats. I depend on technology for daily activities, from waking up with alarms to organizing my schedule with calendars.

Participant 4 replied,

If used responsibly and limited to necessary tasks, technology can lead to more interesting and productive activities. However, over-reliance on technology can complicate life, making simple tasks more dependent on devices. Initially, I felt anxious and dependent on my phone, feeling like a part of me was missing without it. Over time, I have overcome this anxiety and now see my phone as a tool rather than a necessity.

Participant 5 mentioned that "Technology solves many problems by making tasks more efficient and providing solutions. However, it also complicates life by creating dependency and potential for misuse."

Participant 6 replied that technology solves many problems but also creates dependency. Participant 6 stated,

For instance, during a power outage or a system crash, we feel handicapped. It is vital to balance technology use and have occasional detox to manage expectations. Slow internet speeds cause me severe anxiety because I am used to high-speed internet in the corporate world. This dependency creates frustration when expectations are not met.

Participants recognize the dual nature of technology as both a problem-solver and a potential complicator of life. On one hand, technology is appreciated for its ability to streamline tasks, enhance communication, and increase efficiency. On the other hand, there is awareness of its challenges, such as over-reliance, distractions, and the erosion of face-to-face interactions. This nuanced understanding suggests a mature and reflective approach to technology use.

Positive Attitudes. Participants enormously appreciated technology, recognizing its significant contributions to enhancing communication, solving problems, and boosting productivity. This optimistic view underscores the value of technology in various aspects of their lives. For many, digital tools facilitate more efficient workflows, enable better connectivity with others, and provide solutions to everyday challenges. This favorable attitude reflects a broader acceptance of technology as a beneficial and integral component of modern living, highlighting its role in improving personal and professional experiences.

Negative Attitudes. Despite acknowledging the benefits of technology, participants also voiced considerable concerns regarding its potential drawbacks. Technological dependence, distractions, and privacy concerns were prominent, revealing a more nuanced and complex relationship with digital tools. Dependence on technology can lead to decreased focus and productivity, while distractions from constant connectivity may impact overall well-being. Privacy concerns further complicate the picture, as individuals worry about the security of their personal information in an increasingly digital world. These negative attitudes illustrate the challenges associated with balancing the advantages of technology against its potential downsides.

Impact of Device Usage on Work

Participant 7 replied,

> During work time, I minimize personal use, focus on professional tasks, and limit personal communication. I use work-related apps rather than social media. For a class time, I restrict phone use to focus on lectures and class activities, using it only for educational apps, note-taking, and communication-related to classwork or group projects.

Participant 8 mentioned, "I do not use my phone much during work or class time, only for two-step authentication or emergency calls. If there is an issue at work, they contact me through Teams on my phone."

Participant 9 said, "I have completed my studies and will discuss work. I minimize personal use, focus on professional tasks, and use work-related apps and tools during work. I mainly use email and messaging apps for work and client communication."

Participant 10 replied, "During work or class, I limit my phone use to essential tasks like responding to important messages and using productivity apps. I avoid social media and entertainment apps to stay focused."

Participant 11 mentioned, "I rarely use my mobile phone during work. I take breaks every hour to check messages or emails, ensuring my work is not impacted by mobile usage."

Participant 12 replied, "During work, I limit my phone usage to essential tasks to avoid distractions. I put my phone on Do Not Disturb mode during work hours to stay focused."

Maintaining a work-life balance is a priority for many participants, who deliberately separate their work and personal lives through device usage. For example, some participants choose not to receive work emails on their phones to avoid being disturbed outside work hours. This conscious effort to create boundaries between work and personal life suggests a growing awareness of the need to protect personal time in a digitally connected world.

Positive Work Impact. The study revealed that participants perceive technology as having a substantial positive impact on their work. Activities like internet browsing, listening to music, and managing email were highlighted to enhance productivity. These technological tools help streamline work processes by providing quick access to information, facilitating communication, and creating an environment conducive to focus and efficiency. Participants appreciated how these elements contribute to better management of their professional tasks, indicating that technology is a valuable asset in improving work performance and achieving organizational goals.

Multitasking. The ability to multitask using devices was highly valued among participants, underscoring their view of these tools as indispensable for managing multiple responsibilities efficiently. Devices such as smartphones and laptops enable users to switch between various tasks seamlessly, allowing them to handle concurrent activities without significant interruptions. This capability is crucial in a fast-paced work environment where juggling different responsibilities is often necessary. Participants' emphasis on multitasking highlights the importance of technology in supporting their ability to balance and manage a diverse range of tasks effectively.

Interpretation of Study Findings

The interpretation of the findings provides insights into how AI-powered technology influences young adults' communication habits and productivity. These interpretations highlight the significance of these technologies in both personal and professional spheres.

Communication Efficiency

Phones and Laptops as Communication Hubs. The strong preference for phones and laptops highlights their pivotal role as central communication hubs in the lives of young adults. These devices are highly valued for their portability and versatility, enabling users to seamlessly integrate various communication methods such as email, social media, and instant messaging. Their ability to support multiple forms of communication makes them indispensable tools for staying connected across diverse contexts, from personal interactions to professional collaborations. This centrality reflects how essential these devices have become in managing and maintaining relationships in today's digital age.

Mobile phones depend highly on internet activities, including browsing, social networking, GPS navigation, and media consumption. The portability of smartphones makes them the go-to device for on-the-go tasks, highlighting the centrality of mobile technology in participants' lives. This dependency suggests that mobile phones are essential for maintaining daily routines and staying connected.

Instant Messaging and Real-Time Communication. The prevalent use of texting and apps like WhatsApp underscores a broader societal shift towards instant, real-time communication. These methods facilitate rapid exchanges and immediate responses, which are increasingly preferred in personal and professional settings. The efficiency of instant messaging allows for quick problem-solving and continuous engagement, aligning with the fast-paced nature of modern communication. This trend highlights a growing preference for immediacy and flexibility, reflecting the evolving expectations around interacting and communicating.

Participants vastly prefer streaming content over downloading, which reflects the broader trend of moving away from physical storage to cloud-based services. Media sharing is done through messaging apps like WhatsApp and cloud services like Google Drive, indicating a preference for convenient and instant access platforms. This trend also points to an increasing comfort with digital ecosystems that facilitate easy sharing and consumption of media.

Productivity and Multitasking

Enhancing Work Performance. The study highlights that technology profoundly impacts work performance, reflecting its deep integration into participants' daily routines. Devices such as smartphones and laptops enhance productivity by facilitating various work-related activities. For instance, internet browsing enables efficient research and access to information, while music helps improve concentration and focus. Email communication streamlines interactions and ensures timely exchanges. Together, these technological tools support various aspects of work tasks, demonstrating their crucial role in enhancing efficiency and productivity in the workplace.

Importance of Multitasking. Participants highly valued multitasking ability, underscoring modern devices' significance in concurrently managing multiple responsibilities. In today's fast-paced environment, where young adults frequently juggle various roles and tasks, the capability to seamlessly switch between different activities is essential. Devices with multitasking features allow users to handle several responsibilities efficiently, contributing to better time management and overall performance. This ability to multitask effectively highlights the indispensable nature of technology in navigating the complexities of contemporary work and personal life.

Balancing Benefits and Drawbacks

Navigating Technology Dependence. Although technology provides numerous advantages, concerns about dependence and distractions indicate that young adults are conscious of the potential downsides of excessive reliance on digital tools. This awareness of technology's dual impact underscores the importance of developing strategies that leverage its benefits while addressing its risks. Implementing practices that promote mindful usage, set boundaries, and encourage periodic breaks is crucial. Individuals can harness technology's advantages without falling prey to its potential pitfalls, leading to a more balanced and productive engagement with digital tools.

Participant 6 responded, "Slow internet speeds cause me severe anxiety because I am used to high-speed internet in the corporate world. This dependency creates frustration when expectations are not met."

Participant 14 mentioned, "I feel anxious when there are internet outages or server issues, especially when facing deadlines. Dependence on technology for daily tasks can be stressful when systems fail."

Participant 15 said, "I feel dependent on technology but not anxious about it. I can adapt if technology were to disappear, but currently, it is integral to my daily routine."

Privacy Concerns. The growing concern about privacy reflects an increased awareness of data security issues in an era where technology is deeply embedded in daily life. As digital tools become more prevalent, ensuring robust privacy and data protection is paramount. Users are increasingly vigilant about how their personal information is handled and protected. Organizations must prioritize implementing strong security measures, regularly updating privacy practices, and educating users on safeguarding their data. Addressing these concerns helps build trust and ensures that individuals can engage with technology confidently and securely.

Participant 8 replied, "I like content but rarely post or comment due to concerns about legal issues and personal privacy. I prefer to like posts rather than comment."

Participant 10 said technology solves problems by improving communication, automating tasks, and providing access to vast information. "However, it can complicate life by causing distractions, raising privacy concerns, and creating dependency issues."

Participant 12 replied,

> I post photos and updates occasionally to stay connected with friends. I try to be active but balance my engagement due to privacy concerns. The majority of my online friends

are people I know in person. I avoid creating new friends or trusting strangers online as I value my privacy.

Participants expressed concerns about privacy and data security, mainly when using social media or managing sensitive information online. This indicates a heightened awareness of the risks associated with digital life, such as identity theft, data breaches, and the potential misuse of personal information. The caution exhibited by some participants in sharing content or engaging online reflects a growing demand for stronger privacy protections and more secure digital environments.

Implications of the Study

The study's implications extend to various domains, including communication strategies, workplace productivity, and technology management. Participants heavily integrate various technologies into their daily lives. They use various devices like laptops, desktops, smartphones, and tablets for different tasks. This highlights technology's pervasive role in managing personal and professional activities, showing that participants are accustomed to a multi-device environment where each device has a specialized role.

The differentiation of device usage based on context (work, personal, academic) is prominent among participants. For work, laptops and desktops are preferred for their ability to handle complex tasks, such as email communication, document management, and multitasking. Smartphones are favored for personal use due to their convenience and portability, enabling quick access to communication apps, social media, and other personal activities.

For Communication

Continued Innovation in Mobile and Laptop Technologies. The strong preference for phones and laptops underscores the necessity for ongoing technological advancements. Future developments should enhance their communication capabilities to better meet user needs. This could involve integrating new features that improve connectivity and user experience, such as advanced communication tools, better battery life, and more intuitive interfaces. By focusing on these areas, manufacturers can ensure that mobile and laptop technologies continue to evolve in ways that align with users' expectations and demands, ultimately leading to more efficient and enjoyable interactions with their devices.

Real-Time Communication Tools. The prevalent use of instant messaging apps like WhatsApp highlights the importance of real-time, asynchronous communication tools in today's digital landscape. Future communication tools should emphasize features that facilitate seamless, immediate interactions while accommodating flexible schedules and varying time zones. This trend reflects a broader societal shift towards more instantaneous and adaptable forms of communication. Innovations in this space might include improved messaging capabilities, enhanced multimedia sharing, and features supporting synchronous and asynchronous communication. By focusing on these aspects, developers can create tools that align with the evolving needs of users who value immediacy and flexibility in their interactions.

For Workplace Productivity

Integrating Technology in Work Routines. The positive impact of technology on work-related tasks highlights its potential to enhance productivity significantly. To fully capitalize on these benefits, organizations should invest in comprehensive training programs that enable employees to utilize technological tools effectively. These programs should focus on integrating technology into daily work routines, ensuring that employees are familiar with the tools and adept at using them to streamline their tasks and processes. By providing the necessary training and support, organizations can maximize the efficiency and effectiveness of their workforce, ultimately leading to improved performance and productivity.

Developing Multitasking Features. As multitasking becomes increasingly crucial in the modern work environment, a growing opportunity exists to develop tools and features that facilitate seamless task switching. Innovations in user interface design can significantly enhance multitasking capabilities, making it easier for users to manage multiple tasks concurrently without experiencing disruptions. By focusing on creating more intuitive and user-friendly interfaces, developers can help users navigate complex workflows more efficiently. This could involve features like split-screen views, enhanced task-switching shortcuts, or advanced notification management systems, all of which contribute to a more streamlined and productive work experience.

For Technology Management

Promoting Balanced Technology Use. The increasing dependence on technology and the potential for distractions highlight the importance of fostering a balanced approach to its use. Employers and educators are responsible for implementing guidelines that encourage healthy technology habits. This could include incorporating structured breaks into the workday or designating specific "tech-free" periods where employees or students can disconnect from digital devices. By promoting these practices, organizations can help individuals manage their technology use more effectively, reducing the risk of burnout and enhancing overall productivity and well-being.

Addressing Privacy Concerns. With growing concerns about privacy, organizations must prioritize robust security measures that protect personal information. Participants' worries about privacy underscore the need for comprehensive education on safeguarding data in a digital environment. Organizations should provide regular updates on data protection practices, ensuring users know the latest security protocols and tools to enhance their privacy. By taking these steps, organizations can build trust and confidence among users, assuring them that their personal information is secure and their privacy is respected.

Adapting Communication Strategies

To effectively engage young adults in the workplace, it is crucial to tailor communication strategies to align with their preferences. This can be achieved by incorporating a blend of direct and digital methods. Young adults often favor digital communication platforms like instant messaging, emails, and social media, but they also appreciate face-to-face interactions when discussing more complex or sensitive topics. Organizations can create a more engaging and productive work environment by understanding and responding to their communication preferences.

Implementing real-time feedback loops is essential for maintaining effective communication in the workplace, particularly with younger employees. By continually adapting communication practices based on employee responses and preferences, organizations can ensure that their messages are received, understood, and acted upon. Real-time feedback allows for immediate adjustments, creating a dynamic and responsive communication system that keeps pace with the evolving needs of young adults.

Leveraging social media and collaborative platforms is a powerful way to engage younger employees. These tools resonate with the communication habits of young adults, who are accustomed to using them for personal and professional interactions. Organizations can foster a more connected and collaborative environment by integrating these platforms into workplace communication strategies. This approach meets young employees where they are most comfortable and encourages active participation and engagement.

Maintaining transparency and inclusivity in communication is vital for creating an environment where young adults feel heard and valued. Transparent communication ensures that all employees, regardless of age or experience, have access to the same information, fostering trust and openness. Inclusivity, on the other hand, involves actively seeking out and considering the perspectives of young adults, ensuring that their voices contribute to decision-making processes. These practices help build a workplace culture where young adults feel respected and empowered.

Supporting Multitasking and Flexibility

Recognizing and supporting the multitasking capabilities of young adults is essential in today's dynamic work environment. Organizations can accommodate younger employees' fast paced and varied work habits by providing flexible communication and work options. Flexibility allows them to manage multiple tasks simultaneously, balancing their work responsibilities with personal commitments. Offering options such as remote work, adjustable hours, and various communication channels empowers young adults to work in ways that suit their preferences and enhance productivity.

Ensuring that communication platforms are designed for seamless task switching without causing significant interruptions is crucial. Young professionals often juggle multiple projects and responsibilities, so having the ability to move between tasks smoothly is critical to maintaining efficiency. Platforms that minimize disruptions and allow for quick transitions between different modes of communication help keep momentum going, ensuring that productivity is not compromised when shifting focus from one task to another.

Implementing tools that integrate across various devices is vital for enabling young adults to manage their tasks efficiently in different environments. Since young professionals are frequently on the move, accessing tools that work seamlessly on smartphones, tablets, and computers is critical. These integrated tools allow continuous workflow in the office, at home, or on the go. By supporting their ability to work across multiple devices, organizations can help young adults stay organized and productive, regardless of location.

Encouraging a work culture that values adaptability is essential for helping employees, particularly young adults, prioritize tasks based on their unique workflows and needs. In an adaptable work environment, employees can choose how they approach their tasks, allowing them to manage their time and resources more effectively. This flexibility boosts productivity and promotes a sense of ownership and responsibility among young adults, as they can align their work practices with their strengths and preferences.

Addressing Mental Health and Wellbeing

A few participants mentioned using technology to manage their health, such as using apps for fitness tracking or medical appointments. This points to an increasing use of technology for personal health management, reflecting broader trends in digital health and wellness. However, the potential for technology to disrupt sleep patterns or contribute to stress was also hinted at, suggesting that while technology can enhance well-being, it can pose risks if not managed carefully.

Acknowledging the potential mental health impacts of constant connectivity and digital overload is crucial in today's increasingly digital workplace. Young adults, who are often expected to be always available and responsive, can experience significant stress and anxiety from the pressure to remain connected at all times. Recognizing these challenges is the first step in creating a supportive work environment that prioritizes mental well-being. By addressing the risks associated with digital overload, organizations can help mitigate its effects and foster a healthier, more balanced approach to work.

Offering resources and support for managing digital stress is essential to promoting mental health in the workplace. Programs such as mindfulness sessions, stress management workshops, or designated "tech-free" times can provide young adults with the tools they need to cope with the pressures of constant connectivity. These resources offer opportunities to unplug and recharge, reducing the risk of burnout and helping employees maintain a healthier relationship with technology. By making such support readily available, organizations demonstrate a commitment to the well-being of their employees.

Promoting a balanced approach to digital communication is critical to preventing burnout among young adults. Encouraging regular breaks from screens, whether through scheduled downtime or by setting clear boundaries around work hours, helps employees disconnect and recharge. This balance is vital in a culture where the lines between work and personal life can easily blur, leading to exhaustion. By advocating for a mindful approach to digital communication, organizations can create an environment where employees feel empowered to take necessary breaks without fearing falling behind.

Providing education on healthy digital habits empowers young adults to maintain their well-being while staying connected. Workshops or training sessions focused on setting boundaries, managing screen time, and recognizing the signs of digital fatigue can equip employees with the knowledge they need to navigate the digital world effectively. By fostering awareness around the importance of digital health, organizations can help young adults develop habits that support their mental and physical well-being, ensuring that they remain productive and engaged without compromising their health.

Limitations of the Study

While the study provides valuable insights, several limitations should be considered when interpreting the findings. These limitations include the sample size and demographics, which may not fully represent the broader population. Additionally, the self-reported nature of the data could introduce bias, potentially affecting the accuracy of the results.

Sample Size and Demographics

The study's sample size of 15 participants, all aged between 18 and 25 and residing in Torrance, California, presents certain limitations of the findings. This specific demographic focus may not fully capture young adults' diverse experiences and perspectives from different geographic locations or socio-economic backgrounds. The results may reflect the particular context of this small, localized group rather than offering insights applicable to a broader population. As such, while the study provides valuable insights into the experiences of this specific cohort, its conclusions should be interpreted with caution when considering their applicability to young adults in other regions or with different backgrounds.

The chosen sample of 15 participants, all within the age range of 18 to 25, exhibits another significant demographic characteristics that influence the study's outcomes. A vital limitation of the study is the homogeneity in ethnicity, as most participants belong to the Asian ethnicity, primarily hailing from India. Next are Kenya, Nigeria, Mexico, and America. Most of them are enrolled in graduate programs related to their fields of study, such as engineering, computer science, and business, and they are concurrently working in study-related jobs or internships.

Data Collection Method

The reliance on audio-only Zoom interviews in the study may have constrained the depth of the data collected. While this method offers convenience and accessibility, it lacks the richness of face-to-face interactions, where non-verbal cues and body language are crucial in providing additional context and insights. Without visual elements, some subtleties and nuances of participants' responses might be missed, potentially impacting the overall depth and quality of the data. As a result, the findings might not fully capture the complexity of participants' experiences and perspectives, highlighting the need for methods that incorporate visual and non-verbal communication to enrich data collection.

Use of Berlo's SMCR Model

The study utilized Berlo's SMCR model to analyze communication processes. While this model provides a foundational framework in communication theory, it may not fully address the complexities of modern digital communication. The SMCR model, which focuses on the Sender, Message, Channel, and Receiver, is primarily designed for linear communication processes and does not account for the multifaceted nature of contemporary digital interactions. For instance, it does not consider the simultaneous use of multiple communication platforms or the dynamic real-time feedback loops characteristic of today's digital communication landscape. As such, while the SMCR model offers valuable insights, its limitations highlight the need to integrate additional models or frameworks to understand modern communication practices' nuances better.

Transferability

Although the findings are specific to young adults aged 18 to 25 in Torrance, California, they are likely relevant to similar urban populations with high technology usage. The trends in device usage and communication preferences provide insights that can be applied to other regions or among different age groups with comparable characteristics. This transferability allows researchers to use these findings as a reference point for studies conducted in analogous environments or demographics, contributing to a broader understanding of technology's impact on communication and work habits in similar contexts (Wilkes et al., 2018).

Applicability to Broader Research

The study contributes meaningfully to the broader literature on communication and technology use. By employing a qualitative analysis approach and utilizing Python's NLP tools, the research provides a robust framework for exploring these topics. This methodological approach can be adapted in other research settings or with different populations, offering a flexible tool for analyzing communication patterns and technology interactions. The insights gained and the analytical techniques applied can thus inform and enhance studies across diverse contexts, broadening the scope and impact of research in the field.

Recommendations for Future Research and Business

This study focuses on young adults aged 18 to 25 living in Torrance, California. The following recommendations are suggested for further research.

Broader Demographic Studies

Future research should include a more diverse sample, encompassing participants from different age groups, geographic locations, and socio-economic backgrounds. This expansion would provide a more comprehensive understanding of technology use across various demographics.

Longitudinal Studies

Tracking Changes Over Time: Longitudinal studies could offer valuable insights into how technology usage and attitudes evolve. Such studies would help identify trends and shifts in communication habits, particularly as new technologies emerge and integrate into daily life.

Mixed-Methods Approaches

Integrating qualitative and quantitative research methods could provide a more nuanced understanding of the impact of AI-powered devices. Quantitative data could validate qualitative findings, while qualitative insights could offer depth and context to quantitative results.

Focus on Specific Technologies

Future research could focus on the impact of particular technologies or applications, such as social media platforms, productivity tools, or AI-based personal assistants. This approach would allow a more detailed exploration of how these tools influence user behavior and communication patterns.

Impact of AI on Different Sectors

Expanding research to explore the impact of AI-powered devices in various professional sectors, such as education, healthcare, or finance, would provide industry-specific insights. Understanding how technology shapes work practices and communication in these fields could inform strategies for integrating AI more effectively.

Recommendations for Practice

In addition to recommendations for future research, the study's findings suggest several practical applications that could benefit organizations and individuals.

Invest in Modern Communication Platforms

Organizations should prioritize adopting and maintaining up-to-date communication platforms that address various communication needs, from formal meetings to casual interactions. These platforms should be designed to be user-friendly and accessible across various devices, ensuring they cater to the diverse needs of employees. By investing in such versatile and adaptable tools, organizations can enhance collaboration, streamline communication, and improve overall efficiency in the workplace.

Organizations should integrate modern technology into Berlo's Communication Model to improve effectiveness. This involves optimizing the model's components—sender, message, channel, and receiver—to align with today's digital communication environment. By adapting the model to include contemporary communication tools and practices, organizations can enhance the clarity and impact of their messages, ensuring that all elements of the communication process are well-suited to current technological standards and user expectations.

It is essential for organizations to continuously evaluate the effectiveness of their communication platforms and the application of Berlo's model. Regular assessments allow organizations to identify areas for improvement and make necessary adjustments to keep up with evolving communication trends and employee preferences. By staying attuned to technological advancements and changing needs, organizations can maintain effective communication strategies and ensure that their tools and models remain relevant and impactful.

Foster an Inclusive Communication Culture

Creating an inclusive communication culture involves respecting and accommodating diverse preferences. Encouraging open dialogue and feedback can help organizations continuously improve their communication practices, ensuring they remain effective and inclusive.

Implement Training Programs

Providing ongoing training on digital literacy and practical communication skills is essential. Training programs should also address the ethical use of technology, privacy concerns, and strategies for managing digital overload, helping employees navigate the complexities of modern communication tools.

Monitor and Adapt Communication Policies

Communication policies should be regularly reviewed and adapted to align with evolving technologies and employee needs. Organizations should use employee feedback to inform policy changes, ensuring they remain relevant and practical in a rapidly changing technological landscape.

Promote Responsible Technology Use

Encouraging responsible technology use involves setting boundaries for device usage during work hours or meetings to minimize distractions. Resources and support for managing digital stress, such as mindfulness programs or designated "tech-free" times, can help employees maintain a healthy balance between productivity and well-being.

Summary

This study offers significant insights into the role of AI-powered technology in the lives of young adults aged 18 to 25, with a particular focus on their communication habits and productivity. The findings highlight the importance of these technologies in both personal and professional contexts while also addressing the potential drawbacks, such as dependence, distractions, and privacy concerns.

The study underscores the need for continued research into the evolving relationship between technology and its users, especially as AI and other advanced technologies become more deeply integrated into everyday life. Addressing the limitations of this study and expanding the research scope will contribute to a more comprehensive understanding of the impact of AI-powered technology on society.

Overall, the study's objectives were achieved, providing a solid foundation for revising traditional communication models, such as Berlo's SMCR model, to better suit the modern digital communication landscape. By integrating context, feedback loops, multimedia, and digital channels and addressing generational and cultural differences, organizations can ensure effective communication, enhance productivity, and support the well-being of young adults in the workplace. Embracing these strategies will enable businesses to create a dynamic and inclusive work environment that leverages the benefits of AI-powered technology while mitigating potential drawbacks.

www.ingramcontent.com/pod-product-compliance
Lightning Source LLC
Chambersburg PA
CBHW071447230926
51846CB00001B/372
* 9 7 8 7 3 6 7 3 1 4 9 8 8 *